**Gujarat**

*Governance for Growth and Development*

# Gujarat

*Governance for Growth and Development*

BIBEK DEBROY

ACADEMIC FOUNDATION
NEW DELHI

www.academicfoundation.com

First published in 2012
by

**ACADEMIC FOUNDATION**
4772-73 / 23 Bharat Ram Road, (23 Ansari Road),
Darya Ganj, New Delhi - 110 002 (India).
Phones : 23245001 / 02 / 03 / 04.
Fax : +91-11-23245005.
E-mail : books@academicfoundation.com
www.academicfoundation.com

*Disclaimer:*
The findings/views/opinions expressed in this book are solely those of the author and do not necessarily reflect the views of the publisher.


Photographs in the book have been provided by the author.

Cataloging in Publication Data--DK
Courtesy: D.K. Agencies (P) Ltd. <docinfo@dkagencies.com>

**Debroy, Bibek.**
Gujarat : governance for growth and development / Bibek Debroy.
p. cm.
ISBN 9788171889815

1. Gujarat (India)--Economic policy. 2. Gujarat (India)--Social policy. I. Title.

DDC 338.95475 23

Typeset by Italics India, New Delhi.
Printed and bound in India.

# Contents

# Acknowledgements

I COULD HAVE BASED MYSELF IN DELHI and written this book. I consciously decided not to do so. There are plenty of people in Delhi who know about Gujarat, or profess to do so. I could have talked to them. I consciously decided not to do so. Instead, I decided to travel in Gujarat and talk to people there. By people in Gujarat, I do not mean only those who work for the government in Gandhinagar. Yes, I did talk to such people. But I also crisscrossed the state by road, from east to west and north to south. Excluding the extreme northern districts of Banaskantha and Patan, there is no Gujarat district I have not been to. I have travelled more in Gujarat than I have in my own state of West Bengal.

Everywhere I went, I talked to people, whoever I met. And uniformly, everyone was hospitable and enthusiastic. Here was a strange person, a non-Gujarati to boot, who seemed to have this stranger idea about writing a book on Gujarat. If they found this idea odd, they did not show it. Instead, they welcomed me with delight and talked about their achievements with pride. That pride and enthusiasm was infectious and began to infect me. In every part of the country, there are disgruntled people, dissatisfied with their lot, full of complaints, and it is not as if I have not travelled elsewhere in the country. Compared to that, Gujarat was like a breath of fresh air, and complaints about the government not doing this, or not doing that, were extremely rare. As I have said, I do not know about Banaskantha and Patan. But elsewhere, lives were getting better and they wanted to tell me about that. Whether it was among people who worked for the government, or whether it was among people who did not work for the government, that sense of optimism was pervasive.

My primary acknowledgement is to the people of Gujarat, whom I met, and who freely gave me their time. There are too many to mention and as I sit down to acknowledge my debt, my mind is full of images. I went to eat at a restaurant in Rajkot and asked the owner about the mark of a hare on his logo. We began to chat and he gave me an autographed copy of a Gujarati poem he had written. In Surendranagar district, I went to see a crematorium that had been modernised using MP-LADS (Local Area Development Scheme). The *gram pradhan* insisted that I should accompany him and go and see a neighbouring 12$^{th}$ century temple that was now dilapidated. I went to see a cattle pound in Amreli district and another *gram pradhan* dragged me home, insisting that I could not leave without having lunch with him. Near Bet Dwaraka, a priest took me to a rarely-visited Hanuman temple and told me the story about Hanuman's 'son'. A private developer took me on a tour of the wild ass sanctuary. Another forest guide would not let me go until I had actually seen lions in Gir. Someone proudly showed me the shore-line development in Somnath. Someone else, equally proudly, showed me the private jetties in Dahej. If a NGO (non-governmental organisation) showed me nets being used for horticulture in the Dangs, another NGO showed me milk collection centres in Valsad. Yet another NGO showed me community-wells and water supply schemes. A senior government servant gave me a print from a photograph of coral that he had taken. Another senior government servant gave me a copy of a book that he had authored on archaeological excavations. The list is endless. If this book has a discernible strand of optimism and enthusiasm, that is because, I have merely communicated what I heard and imbibed. This is the story of Gujarat's governance, growth and development, as I heard and understood it. The inputs are not mine. I have essentially performed a reporting function.

If this is the primary debt, there is a secondary one too and that is to the Gujarat Social Infrastructure Development Board Society (GSIDBS). Someone needed to facilitate my extensive travels in Gujarat and when I mentioned the idea of a book to GSIDBS, the reaction was overwhelmingly supportive. Had it not been for GSIDBS and the people of Gujarat, this book would not have materialised.

Clearly, people in Gujarat want the Gujarat story to be told. Therefore, here it is.

20th September 2012 Bibek Debroy

# 1

# A Personal Prologue

THIS IS A BOOK about Gujarat and its story of growth and development, not in some distant past, but in recent years. Before getting into the meat of the book, a personal prologue is necessary. If I do not state it upfront, I am certain to be accused of incomplete disclosure.

In 2009, M.V. Kamath and Kalindi Randeri published a book titled *Narendra Modi, The Architect of a Modern State*.[1] That book has excerpts from an interview of Narendra Modi by Karan Thapar, aired on CNN-IBN. Karan Thapar says, "In the six years that you have been the CM of Gujarat, the Rajiv Gandhi Foundation has declared Gujarat to be the best-administered state. *India Today*, on two separate occasions, declared that you are the most efficient chief minister." The awards to Gujarat, listed in appendices to the book, mention a 'Best State of India' award from RGF (Rajiv Gandhi Foundation) and several awards from *India Today*. For years and years, Dr Laveesh Bhandari of Indicus Analytics and I have been involved in the business of ranking states. There are two of these rankings and people who do not notice subtle differences, often confuse the two. The first is a straightforward descriptive cum factual documentation or ranking of inter-state performance and is done for *India Today* every year, based on assorted variables. It is called 'State of the States'. This does not adopt normative positions on policy, at least directly. The second one is called an economic freedom rating. Based on the tradition of economic freedom, it is based on the premise that individual choice and reduced government intervention, is good for development and growth. Thus, one adopts a position on policy. This was originally published intermittently, but has become an annual feature in the last couple of years. Swaminathan Aiyar has also become a co-author to this exercise now. Whether it is *India Today* or whether it is economic freedom ratings, Gujarat has always been towards the top, sometimes at the top of the league table. To get back to the anecdote, Karan Thapar, M.V. Kamath and Kalindi Randeri got it partly wrong. At that time, I was the Director of the RGICS (Rajiv Gandhi Institute of Contemporary Studies) and functionally, RGICS was independent of RGF. In 2005, Laveesh and I brought out an economic freedom rating and Gujarat was at the top.[2] It was a ranking, not quite an award, and it was done by RGICS, not RGF. And there was the standard academic caveat to the paper, to the effect that the views were those of the authors, not necessarily those of the organisations they were affiliated to. When *India Today* rankings showed Gujarat doing well, feathers were not ruffled. But that RGICS paper ruffled political feathers. The gory details do not matter. The outcome was that I exited from RGICS.

---

1. Kamath, M.V. and Kalindi Randeri (2009). *Narendra Modi: The Architect of a Modern State*. Rupa & Co.

2. Debroy, Bibek and Laveesh Bhandari (2005). *Economic Freedom for States of India*. New Delhi: Rajiv Gandhi Institute for Contemporary Studies and Friedrich Naumann Stiftung. March.

Towards the end of 2011, my wife and I decided to take a vacation in Kutch (Kachchh). Perhaps we were persuaded by Amitabh Bachchan. In any event, we wanted to see what Kutch Mahotsav or Rann Mahotsav was all about. In case you do not know, Kutch is India's largest district, measured in geographical area. Bhuj is the district headquarters and there is an impressive story of resilience and recovery from the earthquake of 2001. For the Rann Mahotsav, people usually stay in tents set up by the government, that is, the tourism department (Tourism Corporation of Gujarat Limited). 'Tents' convey the wrong impression, because they are completely comfortable. However, they are tents in the sense of being temporary structures. They are there for around 45 days, during the duration of the peak tourist season and then they are removed. There are around 450 of these. Why should tourists only come for those 45 days? They might not come for the entire year. But they might turn up outside that slot of 45 days. The area where those official tents are set up is uninhabited for the rest of the time. However, in the northern-most inhabited point there is the village of Dhordo. In the course of our trip, we visited the village. We found a solar-powered and biometric SBI (State Bank of India) ATM there, which worked, in the sense that we were actually able to take money out. We found the Panchayat Bhavan powered by solar power. We found a village resort, managed by the *gram panchayat*. It had 10 *bhungas* (mud-huts) that tourists could stay in. (Two of these obtained a rural artisan award from the state government.) Like the 'tents', *bhungas* should not give you the wrong impression. They are perfectly comfortable, and unlike the government-tents, are permanent structures. You can book online, try it out. Kutch has 10 *talukas* and some are more developed than others, by any socio-economic indicator. We are not talking about the relatively more developed southern *talukas* of Kutch. We are talking about the relatively less developed *talukas* towards the north, such as Bhuj. And we saw similar developments in other villages too, like Hodko. There are several reasons for these developments and we will talk about them in the course of the book. Are these developments likely in any other part of India? I began to wonder and the seed of the book was sown.

The Kamath-Randeri volume is dedicated 'to the five-and-a-half-crore Gujaratis for their resilience and entrepreneurship'. As I subsequently travelled through the length and breadth of Gujarat, east to west and north to south, I was convinced there was a story to be told about this resilience and entrepreneurship. When I told people outside Gujarat that I was writing a book on Gujarat, there were two kinds of reactions. First, Gujarat? Isn't Gujarat all "hype"? I have still not understood this reaction. The word 'hype' is applied to something that is exaggerated and questionable, blown up through a media blitz. It is applied to something that is not real. How can growth figures be 'hype'? Growth figures are objective data, or should be. There is no scope for opinion there, or should not be. What do people mean when they say that Gujarat is 'hype'? Judged by conversations, they mean they have problems and questions about the nature of growth. Isn't vibrant Gujarat all about industry? What about agriculture? What about backward regions? What about backward segments of the population? What about social sectors? Those are legitimate questions about the composition of growth and they should indeed be asked. But I would not have used the word 'hype' in that context. That seems inappropriate. Second, Gujarat? Do not write the book. You will be bracketed, labelled and branded. People will not read it. Without the book being read, some people (a minority presumably) will praise you for the wrong reasons and other people (a majority presumably) will condemn you for the wrong reasons. There is a curious lack of objectivity in reacting to the Gujarat phenomenon, the Gujarat model, if there is one. Because of the anecdote I mentioned earlier, there is an understandable sense of *déjà vu*. So be it, *c'est la vie*.

A close personal friend now works for the government. He told me another anecdote that concerns him. It is not an apocryphal story. It is just that I can not name him. He authored part of a report for the Union government. In the process of documenting state-level reforms, he wrote, 'Gujarat has done...' When he saw the printed document, the sentence had changed to, 'Some States have...' Someone with greater political sense had exercised editorial discretion.

Take another example, this time from the *India Human Development Report 2011*.[3] The Gujarat profile states, "To sum up, it appears that the high growth rate achieved by the state over the years has not percolated to the marginalized sections of society, particularly STs and SCs, to help improve their human development outcomes." As a proposition, this may very well be true and we will examine the proposition later in the book. For the moment, let us stick with the *India Human Development Report*. Incidentally, this has dated and old data, but let us ignore that too. Growth is a function of time. To determine whether growth has had an impact on human development outcomes of STs and SCs, what would any academic do? He/she would look at the human development outcomes of STs/SCs over time. But that is not what this report does. It compares Gujarat's performance on human development outcomes of STs/SCs with all-India averages at a single point in time and deduces growth has had no effect on improvements in these. The incremental improvement or deterioration in human development outcomes of STs/SCs is irrelevant. That is an extremely odd kind of logic.

These examples illustrate the obvious. There is a remarkable lack of objectivity in discussing Gujarat and governance, growth and development there. The

3. Institute of Applied Manpower Research and Planning Commission (2011). *India Human Development Report 2011: Towards Social Inclusion*. Oxford University Press.

economics gets enmeshed in the politics and the politics gets entangled with the economics. While this is perhaps inevitable and unavoidable, this book is about the economics. What has happened in Gujarat? Is there a story there? Why has it happened? Is this is a story that can be replicated elsewhere in India? Is there a lesson for other states? I think there is a replication story. Otherwise, I would not have written the book. And once you have read it, hopefully shorn of biases, you decide.

# 2

# The Growth Story : The Macro Cake and its Distribution

GROWTH IS NEVER an end in itself. It is a means to an end, especially because by growth one typically means growth in GSDP (gross state domestic product). In the context of a country, GSDP is akin to GDP (gross domestic product), the total value of goods and services produced in a country over a fixed time period, typically one year. GDP is not the same as GNI (gross national income), since GNI also includes net factor income from abroad. The principle is no different for a state and GSDP is not necessarily the same as GSI (gross state income). The difference can be important for a state where migration and remittances are major variables. However, having accepted the point, one is stuck, since no credible estimates exist for GSI. One only has figures on GSDP and must accept it as a surrogate indicator. GSDP figures are compiled by Directorates of Economics and Statistics of different state governments. They are then 'vetted' by CSO (Central Statistical Organisation) and finalised. GSDP figures can be in current prices, or in constant prices. If we do not wish to get carried away by inflation, we should focus on constant price numbers. In the present case, this means that everything is expressed in 2004-05 prices.[1] Those CSO numbers are often channelled through Planning Commission and Table 2.1 is based on one such Planning Commission table.[2]

Table 2.2 is from another Planning Commission source, the *Mid-Term Appraisal of the Eleventh Five Year (2007-2012) Plan*.[3] For a reason that will become apparent in a moment, we have focussed only on the Gujarat numbers. Table 2.2's figures are dated, compared to those of Table 2.1, especially for the Eleventh Plan. Finally, Table 2.3 is from the same source as Table 2.1 and we have again focussed only on the Gujarat numbers.[4] It is easy to get bogged down in a maze of figures and statistics. It is also possible to nitpick. Average growth numbers are a function of the kind of average one is using, arithmetic *versus* geometric mean, or even the median. If one is breaking up growth into selected time periods, the figures also depend on the initial and terminal years chosen for the breaking up. While such decisions affect specific growth numbers, often at the decimal point, they do not affect the broad picture.

**Table 2.1**

*Real GSDP Growth Rates (% per year)*

| | 1994-95 to 2004-05 *Average* | 2004-05 to 2011-12 *Average* |
|---|---|---|
| All-India | 6.16 | 8.28 |
| **Gujarat** | **6.45** | **10.08** |
| Bihar | 4.94 | 11.42 |
| Maharashtra | 4.97 | 10.75 |
| Sikkim | 6.30 | 12.62 |
| Tamil Nadu | 5.54 | 10.27 |
| Uttarakhand | 4.61 | 12.37 |
| Chandigarh | 9.61 | 10.78 |
| Delhi | 7.62 | 11.43 |

The first broad-brush story from Table 2.1 is as follows. Compared to 1994-95 to 2004-05, from 2004-05 to 2011-12, real GSDP growth rates have increased, from an all-India average of 6.16 per cent to an all-

1. Numbers prior to 2004-05 are at 1999-2000 prices, but that detail is not terribly relevant.
2. *http://planningcommission.nic.in/data/datatable/0904/tab_103.pdf*
3. *http://planningcommission.nic.in/plans/mta/11th_mta/chapterwise/Comp_mta11th.pdf*
4. *http://planningcommission.nic.in/data/datatable/0904/tab_103.pdf*

India average of 8.28 per cent. Second, with an increase from 6.45 per cent to 10.08 per cent, the increase has been more for Gujarat than for all-India. Third, since 2004-05, there are other states that have also grown fast and Bihar, Maharashtra, Sikkim, Tamil Nadu, Uttarakhand, Chandigarh and Delhi have been highlighted in Table 2.1. That growth story in other states is sometimes used as an argument against the Gujarat growth story and that is a bit strange. After all, Gujarat accounts for an estimated 7.5 per cent of Indian GDP. If all-India averages have gone up that much, it is unreasonable to expect growth has been pulled up by Gujarat alone. I do not think anyone who suggests there is a growth story in Gujarat advocates that line of reasoning. Growth in other states is not an argument against Gujarat's growth either. However, in making inter-State comparisons, there is a legitimate question one should ask. Should small states be compared with large states? Should special category states be compared with non-special category states? Smaller states tend to be more homogeneous, with relatively fewer backward geographical regions and districts. Chandigarh, Delhi, Puducherry, Goa and Sikkim are not quite comparable with larger states. With that caveat, it is also true that there has been a growth pickup in Bihar, Maharashtra, Tamil Nadu and Uttarakhand as well. Fourth, Table 2.2 shows a discernible pick-up in Gujarat's growth performance since the Tenth Plan (2002-2007), the five-year plans being natural periods for breaking up the time-line. It is tempting to argue that there is nothing exceptional in this. Gujarat grew fast during the Eighth Plan (1992-1997) too. While that is true, one should accept that as development occurs, it becomes more difficult to sustain higher rates of growth. Among larger and relatively richer states like Maharashtra, Haryana, Gujarat, Kerala, Punjab, Tamil Nadu and Karnataka, it is more difficult to find sources of growth. Growth tends to taper off. Relatively poorer states like Bihar, Orissa, Madhya Pradesh, Assam and Jharkhand find it easier to catch up. Had historical trends alone provided the momentum for growth, Karnataka should have also grown extremely fast. Fifth, too often, discussions focus on growth trends alone. Moving to a higher growth trajectory is important. But reducing the volatility of growth is no less important. Without computing sophisticated measures of volatility of growth, the trends of Table 2.3 should be obvious enough. Growth rates in Gujarat have become much less volatile.

**Table 2.3**

*Real GSDP Growth Rate in Gujarat*

*(% per year)*

| | |
|---|---|
| 1994-95 | 18.02 |
| 1995-96 | 5.49 |
| 1996-97 | 14.24 |
| 1997-98 | 2.11 |
| 1998-99 | 7.18 |
| 1999-2000 | 1.02 |
| 2000-01 | -4.89 |
| 2001-02 | 8.41 |
| 2002-03 | 8.14 |
| 2003-04 | 14.77 |
| 2004-05 | 8.88 |
| 2005-06 | 14.95 |
| 2006-07 | 8.39 |
| 2007-08 | 11.00 |
| 2008-09 | 6.78 |
| 2009-10 | 10.10 |
| 2010-11 | 10.47 |

**Table 2.2**

*Gujarat's Average Real GSDP Growth Rate*

*(% per year)*

| *Seventh Plan (1985-1990)* | *Eighth Plan (1992-1997)* | *Ninth Plan (1997-2002)* | *Tenth Plan (2002-2007)* | *Eleventh Plan (2007-2012) Expectation* |
|---|---|---|---|---|
| 6.1 | 12.9 | 2.8 | 10.9 | 11.2 |

Given Indian conditions, volatility is fundamentally a function of what has been happening to the agricultural sector and Gujarat's agricultural reforms have cushioned against that downturn.

GSDP is an aggregate indicator, in the sense that it is distributed over a population. In Gujarat's case, Census 2011 showed a population of 60.4 million, with a decadal (2001-2011) rate of population growth of 1.9 per cent a year. Subject to the qualification that this is GSDP and not GSI, per capita GSDP growth is a better indicator than GSDP growth of what has happened to the average resident of Gujarat. However, there is not much point in throwing in more numbers unnecessarily. If real GSDP has roughly grown by 10 per cent between 2004-05 and 2011-12 and the rate of population growth has been roughly 2 per cent, per capita GSDP has approximately grown by 8 per cent. Thus, in constant prices, per capita NSDP (net state domestic product) was Rs 17,227 in 2000-01. It increased to Rs 32,021 in 2004-05 and Rs 52,708 in 2010-11.[5] Because of growth, Gujarat's average resident is better off. However, that is an average. As an argument, it is certainly possible that the distribution has worsened and that the benefits of growth have been unevenly distributed across segments of society. Because of what has been said about reduced volatility of growth, that is unlikely. But it is a proposition worth probing.

Therefore, let us move on to the poverty story. No one denies that poverty is a multidimensional concept. It is no one's case that a minimum level of income or consumption expenditure is the sole criterion for identifying someone as BPL (below the poverty line) or APL (above the poverty line). However, the use of income or consumption expenditure is customary, because it is easier to get data on income or consumption expenditure. The methodology has evolved over time, through the Planning Commission and the present one is based on the recommendations of the Tendulkar Committee. Having done all that, one needs data. Data surface through surveys. And that means the NSS (National Sample Survey) Organisation. NSS does not collect data on incomes, because data on incomes are felt to be unreliable. NSS collects data on consumption expenditure. Unfortunately, NSS does not collect such data every year. More accurately, the larger a sample, the more accurate are the data. And NSS large-samples surface roughly once every five years. We had such large surveys in 2004-05 and 2009-10. Two minor issues should be mentioned. First, as with any household survey, there is underestimation. That is, the aggregate of consumption expenditure collected through a survey like NSS falls short of aggregate consumption expenditure collected through national accounts, that is, CSO. This is not a problem that is typical to India. It happens in every country

5. *http://planningcommission.nic.in/data/datatable/0904/tab_109.pdf*

where surveys are conducted. Second, there is a technical issue of the recall period connected with NSS surveys, namely, the period over which respondents are asked details about their expenditure. Figures are sensitive to the recall period used. However, let us gloss over that.

Table 2.4 shows the Planning Commission's poverty numbers, based on NSS 2004-05 and 2009-10.[6] Let us focus on 2004-05 first. Though the Gujarat numbers are below all-India numbers, the figures are high, especially for rural Gujarat. A fast growing state should not have such high poverty numbers. If a fast growing state has such high poverty numbers, that is clear evidence that growth is not trickling down. Or so one might be tempted to think. "Though Gujarat has a low incidence of income poverty, it is still significant given the high economic growth it has achieved over the years."[7] If this growth is a reference to the growth achieved during the Eighth Plan (1992-1997), one can not quibble. But after that, growth picked up during the Tenth Plan (2002-2007), not during the Ninth (1997-2002). The Ninth Plan was a period of slow growth. For growth to have poverty reduction effects, there must be growth to start with. Since growth picked up in 2002, it is unlikely that poverty reduction effects of growth will show up in a NSS round from 2004-2005. Many assertions about poverty, and human development in general, in Gujarat are based on 2004-05 data. As Table 2.4 shows, NSS 2009-10 reveals a different story. In line with all-India trends, overall poverty and urban poverty have declined. But the real story is in rural Gujarat, where there has been a very sharp drop in poverty, significantly more than all-India trends. In rural Gujarat, the benefits of growth have trickled down. In 2009-10, the BPL number for rural Gujarat was 9.2 million. That's still a large number, but is significantly smaller than the 12.9 million in 2004-05. For the record,

**Table 2.4**

*Gujarat and All-India Poverty Numbers (% Below Poverty Line)*

| | 2004-05 | | | 2009-10 | | |
|---|---|---|---|---|---|---|
| | *Rural* | *Urban* | *Total* | *Rural* | *Urban* | *Total* |
| **Gujarat** | **39.1** | **20.1** | **31.6** | **26.7** | **17.9** | **23.0** |
| All-India | 42.0 | 25.5 | 37.2 | 33.8 | 20.9 | 29.8 |

the urban poverty figure was 4.3 million in 2004-05 and 4.5 million in 2009-2010. While the percentage declined in urban Gujarat, the absolute number of BPL went up marginally. There can be issues about the poverty line, what

6. *http://planningcommission.nic.in/data/datatable/0904/tab_45.pdf*

7. Institute of Applied Manpower Research and Planning Commission (2011). *India Human Development Report*. Oxford University Press.

it measures and what it does not. For example, the Planning Commission's poverty line is primarily based on food, with a little bit thrown in for clothing. This made sense earlier, because it was expected that items like education and health were public goods and would be provided by the government. But that debate about revising poverty lines and constructing multidimensional poverty indices, moving away from straightforward head count ratios, is irrelevant for present purposes. Using the same poverty line, and with the condition that one is not using dated data, poverty has declined, especially in rural Gujarat.

However, one should mention the issue of human development, the *India Human Development Report* having already been cited. Every year, UNDP (United Nations Development Programme) brings out a HDR (Human Development Report). This reflects dissatisfaction with usage of head count ratios as the only indicator of human development. Among other things, HDR has a HDI (Human Development Index). HDI is based on three indicators—education (literacy, gross enrolment ratio), health (life expectancy) and PPP (purchasing power parity) per capita income. The higher the value of HDI, the better it is. Several states have also brought out HDRs and these not only compute HDIs for the individual states, they enable us to pinpoint backward districts and intra-state divergences. It would have been a good idea to look at human development in Gujarat. But there is a problem with doing that. Most state-level HDRs are old, the one for Gujarat itself dates to 2004. The national ones also use dated data. Therefore, while it would have been a good idea to use human development indicators, that is not possible. And if one uses dated data, the conclusions are bound to be misleading. Therefore, in subsequent chapters of this book, we will probe the question of human development, but without computing or estimating human development indicators.

This is the right moment to pause and ask several questions. First, are people willingly poor? Do they not wish to better their lives and improve their standards of living? Assuming otherwise is tantamount to a very patronising attitude towards poor people. At best, there can be a qualification for the old and the disabled and households where the head of the household happens to be a woman. These apart, people in working-age groups do not wish to be poor. Income growth and liberalisation will ensure that such people are no longer poor. Second, even if people do not wish to be poor, they may be stuck because they do not have access to education and skills, health services, market information, technology, financial products, roads, electricity, water, sewage and sanitation. But then, the answer is to efficiently provide these public goods or collective private goods. People may also be poor because they are stuck in subsistence-level agriculture and have no other employment opportunities. Third, there is a danger of looking at the problem of poverty with a distorted lens. In any table of poverty, there will be categories of SCs,

STs, OBCs and Muslims. But are they deprived because they belong to these collective categories? Or are they deprived because they lack access to the public or collective private goods we have mentioned? "Indeed, if anything, the data in this volume provide pretty good evidence that the scheduled castes (SCs) and scheduled tribes (STs) are still particularly disadvantaged in many extraordinary ways. What the numbers do seem to imply are: first, there is a good deal of truth in the old-fashioned story that economic and educational opportunities, more than caste identities, are determinants of access to various goods of poverty."[8] Poverty is an individual household characteristic. By equating it with a collective category like SC, ST or Muslim, we commit a double kind of mistake. We assume that everyone inside this collective category is poor, by virtue of being a member of a collective category. And we also assume that everyone outside this collective category is rich, by virtue of not being a member of this collective category. Neither of these propositions is true.

At one level, per capita GSDP is nothing but the average productivity of a state's inhabitants.[9] To increase it, one needs to increase the efficiency with which a state's natural and human resources are used. World Economic Forum's Global Competitiveness Index (GCI) analyses competitiveness on the basis of 12 pillars—(1) institutions; (2) infrastructure; (3) macroeconomic environment; (4) health and primary education; (5) higher education and training; (6) goods market efficiency; (7) labour market efficiency; (8) financial market development; (9) technological readiness; (10) market size; (11) business sophistication; and (12) innovation.[10] As one moves up the development ladder, successive pillars become increasingly important. While GCI is used for cross-country assessments, it is relevant for inter-State performance also. Stated differently, at low levels of development, growth impulses will primarily come from public institutions (improving property rights, reducing corruption, ensuring judicial independence, improving government efficiency, improving security), infrastructure (transport and energy) and health and primary education, though this should not be interpreted as a complete exclusion of the other pillars. In other words, apart from greater efficiency in use of natural and human resources, there is the matter of institutions. Subsequent chapters of this book probe what Gujarat has done on these.

---

8. Mehta, Pratap Bhanu (2010). "Introduction: Caste, Class and Consumption," in Rajesh Shukla, Sunil Jain and Preeti Kakkar (eds.), *Caste in a Different Mould, Understanding the Discrimination*. NCAER and Business Standard.

9. Since per capita GSDP is GSDP divided by population (and not just the working-age population), per capita GSDP is more accurately the average productivity of the working-age population.

10. *http://gcr.weforum.org/gcr2010/*

Let us now turn to the more controversial question of inequality. Poverty is an absolute concept, while inequality is relative. There is an impression that increases in inequality, real or perceived, are bad. In a paper by Suresh Tendulkar, there is an interesting anecdote about a conference in Bangkok when Manmohan Singh was the Deputy Chairman of the Planning Commission. "After other delegations presented their experiences in managing a market economy, the Chinese vice minister presented an outline of the Chinese reform program. At the end of the presentation, Manmohan Singh, in his usual gentle but forceful tone, asked, "Would not what you are trying to do result in greater inequality in China?" To that the minister replied, with great conviction, 'We would certainly hope so!'"[11] There is a difference between inequality in access to inputs (physical and social infrastructure, financial products and so on) and inequality in outcomes (income). Everyone would like India, and Gujarat, to be equitable. But equity should be interpreted in terms of access to inputs and we should be legitimately upset if there is inequity in that. However, why should there be equality in outcomes? There is a difference between saying that every student should have access to a good school and saying that every student should obtain the same marks. Any period of rapid economic growth results in increased income inequalities. Simon Kuznets argued this out a long time ago.[12]

However, one should not get into too much of a digression. Let us save the issue of inequality in access to inputs for later and focus on inequality in outcomes. The problem is the one mentioned earlier. NSS collects data on consumption expenditure, not income. Inequality based on the distribution of incomes will be higher than inequality in the distribution of consumption expenditure. In addition, NSS surveys do not quite capture the upper tail of the distribution, even for consumption expenditure. Therefore, any inequality measure based on NSS surveys will tend to underestimate the true extent of inequality. But these are constant distortions and biases, constant over a period of time. As such, they should not affect trends and intertemporal comparisons, unless those distortions have also changed over time. There are several aggregate measures of inequality. The Gini coefficient is one such standard measure. The Gini coefficient varies between 0 and 1. The higher the value of the Gini, the more unequal society is. And the lower the value of the Gini, the more equal society is. As with any aggregate measure, the Gini hides shifts in the shape of the curve and these can be quite interesting too. But let us stick with the Gini. Table 2.5 shows what we know about Gujarat's Gini, courtesy

11. Tendulkar, Suresh (2010). "Inequality and Equity during Rapid Growth Process", in Shankar Acharya and Rakesh Mohan (eds.), *India's Economy, Performance and Challenges: Essays in Honour of Montek Singh Ahluwalia*. Oxford University Press.

12. Kuznets, Simon (1955). "Economic Growth and Income Inequality", *American Economic Review*.

the Planning Commission.[13] Subject to all those problems about data and measuring inequality, Table 2.5 does not show any remarkable increase in inequality in Gujarat, either rural or urban. The inequality numbers are very close to all-India trends and as with all-India trends, have been almost flat over time. In fairness, one should not have one's cake and eat it too. I have earlier said that growth took off in 2002 and one should not use NSS data for 2004-05. I cannot now turn around and say, using 2004-05 data, that there has not been any increase in inequality. That is a fair criticism, but there is a problem. Using 2009-10 data, Planning Commission has not worked out Gini coefficients. Indeed, Planning Commission also describes the 2004-05 Gini coefficients as 'unofficial' estimates.

**Table 2.5**

*Gujarat and All-India Gini Coefficients*

| *Year* | *All-India* | | *Gujarat* | |
|---|---|---|---|---|
| | *Rural* | *Urban* | *Rural* | *Urban* |
| 1973-74 | 0.28 | 0.30 | 0.23 | 0.25 |
| 1977-78 | 0.34 | 0.34 | 0.29 | 0.31 |
| 1983 | 0.30 | 0.33 | 0.25 | 0.26 |
| 1993-94 | 0.28 | 0.34 | .24 | 0.29 |
| 1999-2000 | 0.26 | 0.34 | 0.23 | 0.29 |
| 2004-05[14] | 0.25 | 0.35 | 0.25 | 0.32 |

The only way of handling this problem is to use someone else's estimates. Among those who work on poverty and inequality, Surjit Bhalla is one of the best known names. Surjit Bhalla shared his estimates for 2009-10 with me. These will be published in a forthcoming paper.[15] These figures are not quite comparable with the ones in Table 2.5 and the difference between Bhalla and the Planning Commission lies in the way they construct price indices to deflate nominal consumption figures into real consumption. That is also the reason why Surjit Bhalla does not have an all-India Gini. According to Surjit Bhalla's numbers, the Gini coefficient in Gujarat in 2009-10 was 0.30. Despite the lack of comparability, this does not show an enormous increase in inequality in Gujarat in the period of high growth. So that we have some kind of benchmark, in those Bhalla estimates, in 2009-10, Delhi had a Gini coefficient of 0.36 and Chandigarh of 0.38. Gini coefficients

13. *http://planningcommission.nic.in/data/datatable/0904/tab_49.pdf*

14. These are the MRP (mixed reference period) numbers. There are some marginal differences with the URP (uniform reference period) numbers.

15. Bhalla, Surjit (forthcoming). *Growth and Inequality, Indian States, 1983-2009.*

tend to be relatively stable over long periods of time. Considering that these are for consumption expenditure and based on NSS, a figure approaching 0.40 represents high levels of inequality in India and such increases have occurred in states that are more urbanised. Urban inequality has increased faster than rural inequality, one reason for the increases in places like Delhi and Chandigarh. In states that have large rural populations, inequality increases are more muted. But to return to the point, there is no evidence of any increase in inequality in Gujarat and that is largely because of what has happened to rural Gujarat and the agriculture story. We will examine

agriculture in a subsequent chapter. And other issues related to inequality, such as STs/SCs/Muslims or regional deprivation, will also be examined in subsequent chapters.

For the moment, at the end of this chapter, the messages are these. There has been high growth since 2002. That growth has resulted in a sharp drop in poverty, particularly in rural Gujarat. There is no evidence of any increase in inequality in the distribution of consumption expenditure. Those are objective statistical facts that cannot, and should not, be disputed.

# 3

# Fiscal Consolidation

"VAST AND DEEP RIVERS—swelling and impetuous—charming pleasure-gardens by the river banks, putting to shame the celestial Nandana-Kânana; amidst these pleasure-gardens rise, towering to the sky, beautiful marble palaces, decorated with the most exquisite workmanship of fine art; on the sides, in front, and behind, clusters of huts, with crumbling mud-walls and dilapidated roofs, the bamboos of which, forming their skeletons, as it were, are exposed to view; moving about here and there emaciated figures of young and old in tattered rags, whose faces bear deep-cut lines of the despair and poverty of hundreds of years; cows, bullocks, buffaloes everywhere—ay, the same melancholy look in their eyes, the same feeble physique; on the wayside refuse and dirt: This is our present-day India!" These are the opening lines of a monograph written by Swami Vivekananda and subsequently translated into English as "The East and the West".[1]

This was written many years ago, but continues to be relevant because of what was said about poverty, inequality and deprivation in Chapter 2. Elimination of deprivation requires public intervention and expenditure, over and above a state's role in providing an enabling environment for private entrepreneurship to bloom and flourish and ensuring rule of law. For instance, there are areas characterised by market failures and externalities, the classic public goods argument. Rural schools, primary health centres in rural areas, drinking and irrigation water, rural roads and electricity generation and transmission, if not distribution, are cases in point. Even if provisioning of such goods and services is outsourced, there may need to be public financing. Alternatively, such goods and services may not be public goods. They may be private or collectively private goods that are merit goods, which need to be subsidised by the state. Development occurs both because of private initiatives and because of state intervention. There is a role for the government and there is a role for the private sector, the latter does not necessarily have to be interpreted as the private corporate sector and includes SMEs (small and medium enterprises), micro enterprises, NGOs (non-governmental organisations), not to mention individuals. However, that state intervention requires resources. At the end of Chapter 2, we ended with the deduction that there has been a rural growth story. Intuitively, that cannot have happened without some form of state intervention and public expenditure. It would have been tempting to jump from that conclusion to a discussion of agriculture. But that would have been like putting the cart before the horse. Therefore, in this chapter, we will focus on fiscal consolidation issues, how resources have been raised and what they are being spent on.

1. *http://www.ramakrishnavivekananda.info/vivekananda/volume_5/vol_5_frame.htm*

It is possible to obtain external, bilateral or multilateral, funding. These can be important in individual sectors. But in an overall sense, external assistance is small and relatively insignificant. The bulk of public resources have to be raised from within the country, the centre or the states. The use of the phrase centre-state is itself symptomatic. It is an expression that is invariably used and reflects a patronising mindset, suggestive of a centre and a periphery. The bedrock of Indian policy is the Constitution of India and nowhere in the Constitution is the expression 'Centre' used, in the sense of the Union government. For example, the Commission that was set up to study relationships between the Union and the states, as a successor to the Sarkaria Commission, with a report submitted in March 2010, was also called a Commission on Centre-State Relations.[2] The point that India is excessively centralised, especially in comparison with a country like China, has often been made.[3] In part, the reason was historical and colonial and this was reinforced by developments after independence. "Looking back and as is well known, in the first three decades after the independence centralization of powers had been accentuated due to various factors such as the predominance of a single political party at the Centre as well as in the States; adoption of planning as a strategy of National development in which investment decisions determined by the Union, albeit through a consultative process, generally set the priorities for State budgets; the system of industrial licensing and control; and nationalisation of major banks. The trend of judicial pronouncements during this period also tended to follow a similar spirit."[4] This is in contrast to a considerable amount of cross-country literature on the benefits of decentralisation. One has to be careful in using the word 'decentralisation', because it can be used to mean different things and not all of these may have anything to do with governance. Within the decentralised governance ambit, there are aspects of political decentralisation, administrative decentralisation, fiscal decentralisation and economic decentralisation. Some arguments in favour of decentralisation are connected to efficient provision of public goods and services and optimal levels of governance, in the sense of economies and diseconomies of scale in providing these public goods and services. Others are linked to making decision-making participative. However, decentralisation is not only about Union-state relations. It is also about decentralisation and devolution within the state and about empowering the third tier of governance. We need not delve into issues that are connected with what the Commission on Centre-State Relations called Constitutional Governance and the Management of

2. *http://interstatecouncil.nic.in/ccsr_report_2010.htm.*

3. See for example, Bardhan, Pranab (2010). *Awakening Giants, Feet of Clay, Assessing the Economic Rise of China and India.* Oxford University Press.

4. *Report of the Commission on Centre-State Relations. http://interstatecouncil.nic.in/volume1.pdf*

Centre-State Relations.[5] But these are important enough for them to be briefly mentioned. First, it has often been the case that when subjects are in the Concurrent List of the Seventh Schedule, the Union has not effectively consulted states, such as before introducing legislation in Parliament. Second, the Inter-State Council has not functioned efficiently. Third, there is a strong case for moving non-tax-related residuary powers from the Union List to the Concurrent List. Fourth, when a Bill has been passed by a State Legislature and sent to the Governor, and the Governor in turn refers it to the President, there are no time limits prescribed and the system is completely open-ended. Fifth, there are issues connected with the appointment and removal of governors, both of which have become politicised. Sixth, discretionary powers of the Governor, including invoking Article 356, should be curbed.[6] Seventh, extending the argument beyond the Inter-State Council, the National Integration Council, the National Development Council, the Planning Commission and the Finance Commission function as extensions of the Union government and have no representation from states. Eighth, the Rajya Sabha is meant to reflect the interests of states, but that territorial link between domicile and election to the Rajya Sabha was severed in 2003.[7] This works against principles of federalism. Ninth, there are issues connected to the all-India services too. Hence, though India is a federation, there are strong unitary biases in this federation.[8]

Let us now turn to the Finance Commission. Irrespective of which state they live in, all citizens of the country should have equitable and equal access to private opportunities and public goods and services. This requires sources of revenue and assignment of public goods to different levels of government. The primary responsibility of the Union ought to be the provision of public goods and services that cut across various states and resolve inter-State issues. For example, on the latter, it can set rules for horizontal competition among states. If one scrutinises the tax and expenditure responsibilities assigned to the Union and states in the Seventh Schedule, one detects an imbalance. On an average, states raise 34 per cent of revenue and incur 58 per cent of expenditure.[9] The 58 per cent expenditure share is also slightly misleading.

---

5. This was the title of the second volume of the report, *http://interstatecouncil.nic.in/volume2.pdf*

6. There are issues connected with Article 356 too. Article 355 also has implications for the deployment of central forces.

7. Through an amendment to the Representation of the People Act.

8. See, Chelliah, Raja (1991). *Towards a Decentralized Polity* (L.K. Jha Memorial Lecture), The Fiscal Foundation and Guhan, S. (1993). "Centre and States in the Reform Process," in Robert Cassen and Vijay Joshi (eds.), *India: The Future of Economic Reform*. Oxford University Press.

9. Govinda Rao, M. and Nirvikar Singh (2005). *Political Economy of Federalism in India*. Oxford University Press. The data in this book are dated, since they are from the late-1990s. However, though the numbers will change if updated, the thrust of the argument will not.

About 15 per cent of state expenditure is on CSSs (centrally sponsored schemes). This requires matching grants from states. Consequently, the free and flexible share in state expenditure is lower than the 58 per cent figure suggests. In addition, state expenditure on CSSs has been increasing over time, so that flexibility in determining expenditure has progressively been declining. The ability of states to finance current expenditure through own revenue is low and has been declining, compounded by an inability on the part of the states to increase capital receipts. Therefore, there has been resort to borrowing and this, and reduction in capital expenditure, has been used to finance current expenditure. The simple point is that there is a 'centripetal' bias in the assignment of tax responsibilities. Ostensibly, this should not matter. Since 2000, after the Tenth Finance Commission, all central taxes are treated as a common divisible pool. However, this is a finite kitty and there are competing claims. This is the standard question of vertical and horizontal equity that all Finance Commissions have been concerned about. States have different fiscal capacities. But the broader background must also be remembered. There is no neat correlation between overall GSDP (gross state domestic product) growth, regardless of its composition, and revenue growth. Nor is the relationship linear. There is a possibility of tapping private sources of funds and Article 293 of the Constitution does allow states to borrow. But this is circumscribed by Article 293(3).[10] This effectively means that, without the permission of the Union, states cannot borrow from the market, as long as they are indebted to the Union. It is impossible to think of scenarios where states will not be indebted to the Union. Thus, borrowing from the market is controlled by the Union. After 1985, overdrafts with RBI (Reserve Bank of India) are also controlled. These are points to be borne in mind when considering Centre-State fiscal concerns. Once the vertical share has been determined, one needs to ensure horizontal equity. Union-state fiscal transfers take place through the Finance Commission, the Planning Commission's flows according to development plans and discretionary transfers through central sector and CCSs. The point to note is that the constitutional mechanism for transfers is through the Finance Commission. Article 280 does not provide for any other channel to distribute the net proceeds of taxes to states. There is no provision in the Constitution for what are called Plan-transfers. These have been justified under Article 282, but the Constitutional legality of this is questionable.[11] Even if this is Constitutionally legal, this cannot have been the spirit of Article 282. In any event, before

10. "A State may not without the consent of the Government of India raise any loan if there is still outstanding any part of a loan which has been made to the State by the Government of India or by its predecessor Government, or in respect of which a guarantee has been given by the Government of India or by its predecessor Government."

11. "The Union or a State may make any grants for any public purpose, notwithstanding that the purpose is not one with respect to which Parliament or the Legislature of the State, as the case may be, may make laws."

1969, such Plan transfers were on the basis of specific schemes. However, with these becoming broad-based and with the Planning Commission increasing in importance, the Finance Commission's transfers are restricted to tax devolution and grants to cover non-Plan current expenditure, with grants-in-aid covered by Article 275 of the Constitution. In any event, the Plan *versus* non-Plan distinction is artificial and prevents one from taking an integrated view, even for the limited purpose of transfers to states. That apart, post-1991, the role of planning itself is questionable. To get back to the point, from the Fourth Finance Commission onwards, right up to the Ninth, grants for Plan expenditure and grants for capital expenditure have been excluded from the purview of the Finance Commission and its terms of reference have been progressively diluted.[12] One therefore needs to abolish the Plan *versus* non-Plan distinction, drastically reduce transfers through the Planning Commission and restore the Constitutional mandate of the Finance Commission. Even when terms of reference have not explicitly excluded Plan and capital expenditure, as has been the case since the Tenth Finance Commission, these have implicitly been excluded. If one reads Article 275, the intention seems to have been that grants-in-aid will be for backward states and a gap-filling exercise will be done. None of this is attempted and there is also lack of transparency in determination of SCSs (Special Category States). If grants-in-aid are based on backwardness criteria like population, should regular Finance Commission transfers have that much of a weight on population?

Let us move on to the Planning Commission, arguments having already been made about reduction in fund flows through the Planning Commission. Transfers routed through the Planning Commission have both discretionary and non-discretionary elements. For non-discretionary transfers, the Planning Commission uses the Gadgil formula, modified as the Gadgil-Mukherjee formula from 1991, though it was first used in 1969. Thirty per cent of available funds are reserved for SCSs. Non-SCSs obtain funds, out of the balance, on the basis of population (60%), per capita GSDP (25%), performance (7.5%) and special problems of these states. Of these, special problems of these states only amount for a 7.5 per cent weight. The point is that for non-SCSs, flows are not based on planned investments, the sectors these investments are in, or the resources available to states. This is not logical. The grant/loan composition is not based on any such analysis either. Non-SCSs obtain 30 per cent as grant and 70 per cent as loans and the reason for this is that this was the actual ratio when the Gadgil formula was introduced. This does not take into account the repayment capacity of

12. That pressure from the Planning Commission was responsible for this dilution is evident from the account given about non-acceptance of the recommendations of the Third Finance Commission. See Chanda, A. (1965). *Federalism in India*. London: George Allen and Unwin.

states or the composition of expenditure. For instances, the implications of spending on human capital, as opposed to physical capital, are quite different. This brings one to discretionary transfers by the Planning Commission through central sector schemes and CSSs. Central sector schemes are few. Most transfers are through CSSs that require matching contributions from non-SCSs. The CSSs have proliferated and at least in the course of the Tenth Plan, the Planning Commission's view was that they should be pruned.[13] That was also the view of the Commission on Centre-State Relations.[14] But no such pruning has been attempted. Other than efficiency, delivery and focus, there are other problems with CSSs too. They encroach on items that are on the State List, or impose centralised templates with rigidities. The 2009 RTE (Right to Education) Act, the earlier SSA (Sarva Shiksha Abhiyan) and RMSA (Rashtriya Madhyamik Shiksha Abhiyan) are instances. In 1996, at a conference of Chief Ministers, it was agreed that all CSSs that impinge on the State List will be transferred to states. But that decision has not been implemented. Because of the matching requirement, the financial burden on states increases. Conditions are imposed on states, often in areas that are the legislative domain of states. CSS transfers are often made to autonomous bodies, bypassing the states. Some CSSs require the creation of a fresh and new bureaucratic system of delivery. In any event, CSSs amount to a unilateral decision by the Union to divert resources that would otherwise have been available to states. Therefore, CSSs should be pruned and more 'untied' funds should be available to states. These need not be completely untied, in the sense that there can be overall guidelines and some indication of the sector for which the funds can be used. Subject to that, states need to have far greater flexibility. The design of CSSs is extremely centralised and is done in Delhi, without any bearing on what a state really needs. With such central templates, it is understandable that implementation will leave a lot to be desired.

Finally, decisions on natural resources are also unduly centralised. Coal, crude oil and gas are examples.

None of these are problems that are specific to Gujarat alone and all States have to reckon with this unnecessary centralisation. The objective is not to enter into a detailed discussion of Centre-State relations. After all, this book is about Gujarat and this chapter is about fiscal consolidation in the state. But it is important to appreciate the constraints under which any state operates.

The fiscal consolidation exercise has a time line. The background is the amendment to the FR (Fiscal Responsibility) Act. The original FR Act of 2005

13. *http://planningcommission.nic.in/reports/articles/ncsxna/ncsax2a.htm.*

14. *http://interstatecouncil.nic.in/volume3.pdf. http://interstatecouncil.nic.in/volume7.pdf* is also relevant.

had a target of reducing the revenue deficit/GSDP ratio to 0 per cent by 31st March 2008 and its maintenance at that level, or transiting to a revenue surplus, thereafter.[15] The fiscal deficit/GDP ratio was to become 3 per cent by 31st March 2009. The public debt/GSDP ratio was to be capped at 30 per cent from 31st March 2008 and outstanding guarantees would be capped according to the provisions of the Gujarat State Guarantees Act of 1963.

The antecedents of reform go back to the 1990s. For example, a SFC (State Finance Commission) was set up in 1992 and it submitted a report in 1994. However, many of those recommendations could not be implemented, primarily because of lack of fiscal space. At that time, states were allowed to negotiate with multilateral institutions for loans that would drive reforms and ADB (Asian Development Bank) negotiated a PSRMP (Public Sector Resource Management Program) with Gujarat government, to be implemented over two years from 1996. In the ADB's words, that $ 250 million loan had the objective of "(i) strengthened state finances and their prudent management, (ii) reformed SOEs[16] contributing to the state economy, and (iii) private sector participation in infrastructure development in the state."[17] Everything that was hoped for could not be accomplished. "Significant exogenous shocks required *ex post* adjustment of the Program's fixed nominal fiscal targets. Revenue generation marginally improved, and the limited expenditure interventions had a limited positive effect. Overall SOE reforms to fully privatize, merge, or close the operations of SOEs have been more effective than those to partially privatize. Corporate governance changes have been less successful. Identifying specific SOEs to be privatized in tranche release conditions was not effective. The reforms to encourage private sector participation in the state's infrastructure development were highly successful, with Gujarat being the first state to enact a law to regulate private sector participation. This act also gave GIDB[18] statutory authority to develop and oversee the state's strategic infrastructure development plans. The establishment of an independent electricity regulatory authority and unbundling of the electricity board provided the foundations for longer term power sector reform, supported by ADB power sector loans in 2000 and 2006. Similarly the unbundling of the maritime board opened the door for considerable private investment in the port sector. Over $5 billion of private capital has been invested in the power, ports, and roads sectors since the late 1990s. A study of the counterfactual, found in the short term that the loan did not lead to any significant improvement in the overall fiscal situation

15. *http://financedepartment.gujarat.gov.in/pdf/fiscal%20act.pdf*

16. State owned enterprises.

17. India: Gujarat Public Sector Resource Management Program, Performance Evaluation Report. July 2007, *http://www.adb.org/sites/default/files/29458-IND-PPER.pdf*

18. Gujarat Infrastructure Development Board.

in Gujarat." The main exogenous shock was the implementation of the recommendations of the Fifth Pay Commission in 1996-97. This adversely affected the finances of all states, not just Gujarat. While the fiscal situation may not have improved that much, some legacies were left, beyond PPPs (public private partnerships) in infrastructure, the Gujarat Infrastructure Act, the Gujarat Infrastructure Fund, the Gujarat Electricity Regulatory Commission and restructuring of PSEs (public sector enterprises). There was simplification of sales tax, goods tax, motor vehicles tax, registration tax and stamp duties. A State Public Finance Reform Committee also submitted a report in 2000. Stated differently, the ground conditions and recommendations for fiscal reforms already existed. Those reforms also made eminent sense. With fiscal consolidation and restructuring, interest costs of market borrowings would be lower than expensive loans from Delhi. The Eleventh (implemented between 2000 and 2005) and Twelfth (implemented between 2005 and 2010) Finance Commission offered an additional opportunity.

Other than rationalisation of indirect taxes, the FR Act also meant that a medium-term fiscal policy statement and a fiscal policy strategy would have to be presented in the legislative assembly, along with the annual financial statement. A few quotes from the 2007-08 statements are indicative of intended reforms.[19] "The State Government's strategy is to increase tax revenue without imposing any new tax and without increasing the present tax rates. Rationalization of the tax-structure of the State continues to be a major priority area. Taxation reforms would continue during the ensuing year aimed at widening the tax base, improving tax compliance and making tax administration more efficient and fair. The process is expected to yield an improved tax to GSDP ratio. After introduction of the Value Added Tax since April 2006, the implementation issues related to VAT administration have largely been addressed to ensure that tax-payers are facilitated. Refund procedures have been streamlined. Rationalization would continue as regards Stamp Duty and Electricity Duty to ensure fewer and moderate rates. Tax on Motor Vehicles would be rationalized. With the above simplifications and rationalizations, it is envisaged that the common man would be benefitted and economic activities would also get the required boost ensuring a wider tax base resulting in better tax buoyancy...The State Government has been attempting to recover the user charges to the extent possible. It is realized that in several areas of service delivery, full recovery of cost is not possible. However, attempts would continue to be made to recover at least the operation & maintenance costs to the extent possible." Prior to VAT (value added tax) in 2006, sales tax on electricity was abolished in 2002 and between 2002 and 2003, motor vehicles tax, entertainment tax, stamp duties

19. *http://financedepartment.gujarat.gov.in/budget07_08_pdf/Fiscal%20Responsibility%20Budget%20Management%20Act-2005%20%28English%29.pdf*

and luxury tax were rationalised. Understandably, on the revenue side, the focus has been on reducing revenue expenditure, not capital expenditure, especially non-Plan revenue expenditure. It is important to flag something that has already been mentioned, the Twelfth Finance Commission's debt swap facility. "The average cost of debt for Gujarat which was 12.10% in 2001-02 is expected to further reduce to 9.33% in the year 2006-07. The average cost of debt for Gujarat which was 12.10% in 2001-02 is expected to further reduce to 9.33% in the year 2006-07. This was achieved mainly due to various measures of debt swap undertaken by the State Government." There was also a cap on guarantees. "Attempts have been made to reduce the guarantees given by the State Government which has resulted in limiting the outstanding Government guarantees at a much lower level than what is fixed in Gujarat State Guarantee Act, 1963. A Guarantee Redemption Fund has been set up to take care of any contingent liabilities arising out of the State Government guarantees. The Guarantee Redemption Fund would continue to be augmented from the guarantee fees received." Finally, "The State Government had taken several initiatives to contain the non-plan revenue expenditure. Some of these measures includes abolition of vacant posts, re-deployment of existing staff so as to avoid filling up of vacant posts, recruitment of essential staff mostly on fixed pay basis, introduction of New Defined Contribution Pension Scheme for employees joining service on or after 1-4-05. These measures have resulted in containing the revenue expenditure, especially the non-plan revenue expenditure during the last 4 years. The State Government would continue to make efforts to contain the growth of revenue expenditure. In addition, the State Government would make attempts to improve the quality of expenditure. As a part of such attempt, the State Government has announced linking release of grants to grant-in-aid institutions to their performance...The State has adopted E-tendering as a substitute to the existing system of tendering for quicker and cost effective means for processing of tender documents. New changes have also been made in financial powers for according administrative sanctions for quicker approval of cases. This would help in improving quality of expenditure and reduce transaction costs." There was something akin to a ZBB (zero-based budgeting) of schemes, with the caveat that if it is a central sector or centrally funded scheme, it is difficult to scrap it, even though a State has to provide a matching contribution.

One should now take a look at the deficit numbers. However, there are some qualifications. First, the global financial crisis, fiscal stimulus and the slowdown in growth adversely affected finances of all states in 2008-09 and 2009-10. Tax devolution from Delhi also suffered. Second, there were the repercussions of the Sixth Pay Commission. Third, there is always a difference between BE (budget estimates), RE (revised estimates) and actuals. Till fiscal year 2009-10, one has actuals. For 2010-11, one has RE numbers and for 2011-12, one has BE estimates. That last statement is partly incorrect, because one now has RE for 2011-12 too and BE for 2012-13. However, that is through State budget documents. In so far as RBI processing of budget numbers is concerned, we are still with 2011-12. As a background, the time line of the original 2005 FR Act was changed through an amendment, as it was for all states. For Gujarat, the revenue deficit/GSDP ratio should become 0 per cent by 2011-12 and retained at that level, or shifted to a revenue surplus thereafter. The fiscal deficit/GSDP ratio should decline to 3 per cent by 2011-12 and retained at that level, or be lower, thereafter. The public debt/GSDP ratio should not be more than 27.1 per cent for the period 2011-12 to 2014-15, in line with the recommendations of the Thirteenth Finance Commission. Guarantees must be capped, in accordance with the Gujarat State Guarantees Act.

**Table 3.1**

*Gujarat's Overall Deficit Indicators (%)*

| *Variable* | *Gujarat* | *Average for Non-Special Category States* |
|---|---|---|
| Revenue deficit/GSDP, average for 2004-2008 | 0.2 | 0.2 |
| Fiscal deficit/GSDP, average for 2004-2008 | 2.6 | 2.7 |
| Primary deficit/GSDP, average for 2004-2008 | 0.0 | 0.0 |
| Revenue deficit/GSDP, 2009-10 | 1.6 | 0.7 |
| Fiscal deficit/GSDP, 2009-10 | 3.5 | 3.3 |
| Primary deficit/GSDP, 2009-10 | 1.5 | 1.4 |
| Revenue deficit/GSDP, 2010-11, RE | 1.1 | 0.5 |
| Fiscal deficit/GSDP, 2010-11, RE | 3.1 | 3.1 |
| Primary deficit/GSDP, 2010-11, RE | 1.3 | 1.2 |
| Revenue deficit/GSDP, 2011-12, BE | -0.1 | -0.1 |
| Fiscal deficit/GSDP, 2011-12, BE | 2.4 | 2.7 |
| Primary deficit/GSDP, 2011-12, BE | 0.6 | 0.8 |

Table 3.1 shows Gujarat's overall deficit indicators. These are based on RBI sources. As I have said earlier, deficit numbers are also available for 2012-2013, on the basis of budget documents. However, the deficit numbers given in budget documents are absolute numbers. The budget papers do not give ratios as shares of GSDP, or projected GSDP numbers. Any projected GSDP number has subjectivity, *ex-ante*. Therefore, Table 3.1 does not incorporate numbers from the 2012-13 budget, since no particular insight is gained from that incorporation. Table 3.1 also gives the average figure for non-SCSs. In that comparison, the fiscal and primary deficit numbers look respectable enough. Historically, the problem has been with the revenue deficit, especially after

2008, both because revenue receipts have been lower and because revenue expenditure has been higher. However, since 2011-12, the revenue deficit numbers have also begun to look respectable and the deficit numbers are marginally better than what the Thirteenth Finance Commission envisaged. While on the aggregate numbers, there is also the target of debt stock/GSDP, meant to be reduced to 27.1 per cent. RBI reports a debt/GSDP ratio of 26.9 per cent in 2010-11 and 26.0 per cent in 2011-12. However, the state government reports a debt stock/GSDP ratio of 22.83 per cent in 2009-2010, 21.98 per cent in 2010-11 and 22.01 per cent in 2011-12. This anomaly is partly a definitional problem and the RBI's focus is on outstanding liabilities. But regardless of the indicator, the Thirteenth Finance Commission targets have been achieved.

That's the overall budgetary position. Within that, a few issues need to be flagged. First, receipts on the capital account are primarily in the form of public debt. For example, in the BE for 2012-13, 99 per cent of capital account receipts are some form or other of public debt. However, one should note that no state, Gujarat included, has control over the small savings component of public debt. Second, capital expenditure is still not as high as it should be. Capital expenditure constitutes 28 per cent of total expenditure. Of course, this statement is subject to qualifications. The differences between capital and revenue, Plan and non-Plan, and even developmental and non-developmental, can be artificial. One of the building blocks of the Gujarat model, so to speak, is to free up space for private sector expenditure in capital formation. One cannot expect capital expenditure, as a share, to increase overnight. While all these qualifications are valid, the statement about capital expenditure should still be made. The bulk (76%) of capital expenditure is developmental, with social services accounting for 55.2 per cent. Of the total expenditure, 66.41 per cent is also developmental. Third, on the revenue receipts side, non-tax revenue is still low, underlining limited movement on PSE reform and implicit subsidies with public utilities being a bit of an exception. Fourth, one still does not which state-level taxes will be eliminated and clubbed with GST (goods and services tax). Pending that, one would have expected land revenue, stamps and registration and taxes on vehicles to account for a much larger share of state taxes than they presently do. Fifth, 63.2 per cent of revenue expenditure is developmental. To the extent this reveals a prioritisation according to sectors, the major ones are education, sports, art and culture and water supply, sanitation, housing and urban development, in that order.

Beyond the mechanical numbers, where does this leave us at the end of this fiscal consolidation chapter? At the risk of sweeping generalisations, three propositions suggest themselves. First, the rigidities of central sector and CSSs have already been mentioned. The fiscal consolidation and fiscal space created has enabled Gujarat to plug the gaps with State-level schemes.

Second, the story isn't that much about increasing public expenditure. It is more about creating an environment for private expenditure. Third, apart from private expenditure, the story is about increasing the efficiency of public expenditure, more bang for the buck, so to speak. We will probe these in later chapters. Fourth, while IT usage in many states has been restricted to treasury management, Gujarat's IFMS (Integrated Financial Management System), working in tandem with the IWDMS (Integrated Workflow and Document Management System), has gone far beyond that. IWDMS automated government functions and processes and in 2007, also won an award for G2G innovations. In addition to treasury management, IFMS makes budget preparation and execution online and this also extends to audit and planning functions. For example, administrative approvals are in place before the budgets is presented, quarterly installments are released in advance and fund flows happen in real time. These governance innovations alone produce much better bang for buck.

# 4

# Physical Infrastructure :
## *Bijli, Pani, Sadak*

THE WORD INFRASTRUCTURE lacks a precise definition. 'Infra' means below. So anything that supports the economic structure or system is infrastructure. While originally, the term was often applied to defence, by the 1970s, it came to be applied to public assets. In particular, there was concern in the US (United States) that the US was losing its competitive edge because of decay in its infrastructure.[1] The US National Research Council sought to pin down the term by essentially providing examples of infrastructure.[2] Infrastructure can be divided into hard and soft infrastructure, the latter encompassing human capital, the social sector, financial services and even the legal system. However, when most people use the term infrastructure, they mean hard infrastructure, that is, physical infrastructure. That is the sense in which the term is used in this chapter as well. We will turn to soft forms of infrastructure in later chapters. Instances of such infrastructure can be found in transport (roads, highways, railways, canals, air and sea ports, mass transit), energy (power, natural gas, mines), water management (drinking and irrigation water, sewage, drainage), communications (postal services, telephones, radio and television transmission, internet) and solid waste management. Most examples of infrastructure people think of will fit into one or the other of these categories.

In 1994, the World Bank's WDR (World Development Report) had the theme of infrastructure for development.[3] Later WDRs have also tangentially touched upon the subject. A few pointers from the 1994 WDR are useful. First, economic infrastructure includes public utilities (power, telecommunications, piped water supply, sanitation, sewerage, solid waste collection and disposal, piped gas), public works (roads, dams, canals) and other transport (urban transport, railways, ports, waterways, airports), what economists often refer to as social overhead capital. Economic infrastructure and social overhead capital are both umbrella terms and share technical features (like economies of scale) and externalities (spillovers from users to non-users). Second, because of natural monopolies and market failures, one has often tended to assume that infrastructure is a public good and must be provided by the public sector. That is no longer necessarily true and there are opportunities for unbundling, facilitated by advances in technology. Third, using cross-country estimates, a 1 per cent increase in the stock of infrastructure is associated with a 1 per cent increase in GDP. Fourth, "Major investments have been made in infrastructure stocks, but in too many developing countries these assets are not generating the quantity

1. See Choate, Pat and Susan Walter (1981). *America in Ruins: The Decaying Infrastructure*. Duke Press Policy Studies.

2. *Infrastructure for the 21st Century*, National Academy Press, Washington, 1987.

3. World Bank (1994). *World Development Report: Infrastructure for Development*. World Bank and Oxford University Press.

or the quality of services demanded...The causes of past poor performance, and the source of improved performance, lies in the incentives facing producers." Fifth, even among the poor, there is a willingness to pay higher user charges, provided that quality of service is ensured. Sixth, efficiency can increase through private sector involvement in management, financing and ownership. "Competition can be introduced directly, by liberalizing entry into activities that have no technological barriers, and indirectly, through competitive bidding for the right to provide exclusive service where natural monopoly conditions exist and by liberalizing the supply of service substitutes." Seventh, even when there are privatisation options, the government will have a role in financing and regulation. The WDR suggested that a 1 per cent increase in infrastructure stock can increase GDP by 1 per cent. The Indian figures that float around are higher. For instance, the National Manufacturing Competitiveness Council formulated a National Strategy for Manufacturing, where it argued that adequate infrastructure can improve GDP growth by a factor of 1.5 per cent, with 1 per cent accounted for by the power sector alone.[4] In some recent speeches, Union Finance Ministers have jacked up incremental GDP estimates from 1.5 per cent to 2 per cent. That thus, is the opportunity cost of lost GDP growth. It may be GDP for India and GSDP for states. But the point remains the same. Inadequate infrastructure means lost growth opportunities.

India is a large and heterogeneous country and there are considerable differences among states and even within states. How does Gujarat perform on infrastructure? There have been attempts to compute infrastructure indices for states. For example, Finance Commissions have been concerned with vertical equity (Centre *versus* State issues) and also horizontal equity (allocations among states). Horizontal equity and horizontal transfers have been made a function of a state's backwardness and physical infrastructure is one of the indicators used in determining backwardness. Whenever such an infrastructure index is constructed, the values depend on the variables included, the weights attached to them and the aggregation formula. Consequently, different indices can show differing results. The Twelfth Finance Commission

4. National Manufacturing Competitiveness Council (2006). *National Strategy for Manufacturing*. March.

grouped States into five categories, on the basis of an infrastructure index constructed by IDFC (Infrastructure Development Finance Company).[5] Goa, Maharashtra and Punjab were 'high'. Gujarat, Haryana, Kerala and Tamil Nadu were 'high middle'. Andhra Pradesh and Karnataka were 'middle'. Himachal Pradesh, Madhya Pradesh, Orissa, Uttar Pradesh, Uttarakhand

5. Ministry of Finance (2004). *Report of the Twelfth Finance Commission (2005-2010)*. November.

and West Bengal were 'lower middle'. And Arunachal Pradesh, Manipur, Meghalaya, Jharkhand, Mizoram, Nagaland, Assam, Chhattisgarh, Sikkim, Tripura, Jammu & Kashmir, Bihar and Rajasthan were 'low'. CMIE (Centre for Monitoring the Indian Economy) has a composite infrastructure index that is based on seven infrastructure heads of transport, energy, irrigation, banking facilities, communication facilities, education facilities and health facilities. The respective weights attached to these heads are 26%, 24%, 20%, 12%, 6%, 6% and 6%. Eleven (11) development indicators are used for these seven heads and these are—(i) surfaced roads per 100 sq km area; (ii) unsurfaced roads per 100 sq km area; (iii) railway route length per 100 sq km area; (iv) percentage of villages electrified; (v) gross cropped area; (vi) bank branches per lakh population; (vii) post offices per lakh population; (viii) telephone lines per 100 persons; (ix) primary schools per lakh population; (x) primary health centres per lakh population; and (xi) hospital beds per lakh population. The reforms started in 1991 and backward states had a backlog of bad infrastructure even before the reforms started. To convey a sense of this historical backwardness and deprivation, Table 4.1 shows this composite development index for major states in 1991. There have also been sporadic efforts, such as that by T.C.A. Anant, K.L. Krishna and Uma Roy Choudhary.[6] This constructed indices of infrastructure availability for 25 Indian states for the period 1985-1990. For this, 24 infrastructure variables are classified into eight sectors—agriculture, banking, electricity, communications, transport, education, health and civil-administration. The first five sectors are referred to as economic infrastructure and the next three as social infrastructure.

**Table 4.1**

*CMIE Composite Development Index, 1991*

| *State* | *Composite Development Index* | *Rank* |
|---|---|---|
| Andhra Pradesh | 104.01 | 10 |
| Assam | 104.39 | 9 |
| Bihar | 91.31 | 13 |
| **Gujarat** | **105.33** | **8** |
| Haryana | 133.12 | 4 |
| Karnataka | 106.12 | 7 |
| Kerala | 162.42 | 2 |
| Madhya Pradesh | 86.66 | 15 |
| Maharashtra | 106.77 | 6 |
| Orissa | 101.45 | 12 |
| Punjab | 171.92 | 1 |
| Rajasthan | 87.27 | 14 |
| Tamil Nadu | 145.62 | 3 |
| Uttar Pradesh | 112.04 | 5 |
| West Bengal | 102.09 | 11 |

The intent is not to get into a digression on how different states perform on physical infrastructure and interstate rankings. The answer depends on what one means by physical infrastructure, what one includes and what one excludes. And the answer also depends on the time line. For instance, whether it was the infrastructure index used by the Twelfth Finance Commission, or the CMIE rankings of Table 4.1, Gujarat was not at the bottom. But nor was it at the very top. It is doubtful that too many people will agree with such a perception today. The GIDB (Gujarat Infrastructure Development Board) was set up under the Gujarat Infrastructure Development Act of 1999. In 2009, GIDB, with CRISIL, brought out a *Blueprint for Infrastructure in Gujarat*. This is known as

6. Anant, T.C.A., K.L. Krishna, Uma Roy Choudhary (1999). *Measuring Inter-State Differentials in Infrastructure*. Delhi: Centre for Development Economics, Delhi School of Economics.

SunEdison
GSECL
ROVAR NARMADA NIGAM LTD

the BIG-2020 report.[7] If one considers this document, there are 12 segments of physical infrastructure that one has in mind: (1) ports: (2) power; (3) roads; (4) railways; (5) aviation; (6) urban infrastructure; (7) urban transport; (8) water supply; (9) industrial parks; (10) information technology; (11) gas; and (12) tourism. Depending on one's perspective and biases, one or the other of these will be regarded as more important.

In terms of impact of connectivity on disadvantaged segments, I am inclined to pick power first. The background is partly the Gujarat Electricity Industry (Reorganisation and Regulation) Act of 2003. This allowed the transfer of assets and liabilities of the former GEB (Gujarat Electricity Board). Generation assets were transferred to GSECL (Gujarat State Electricity Corporation Limited). Transmission assets were transferred to GETCO (Gujarat Transmission Corporation Limited). Four different distribution entities were formed—UGVCL (Uttar Gujarat Vij Company Limited), DGVCL (Dakshin Gujarat Vij Company Limited), PGVCL (Pashchim Gujarat Vij Company Limited) and MGVCL (Madhya Gujarat Vij Company Limited). GUVNL (Gujarat Urja Vikas Nigam Limited) had residuary functions, including that of power trading. GUVNL is the holding company. The Gujarat Electricity Regulatory Commission had been set up in 1998 and was brought under the purview of the Electricity Act of 2003. Generation became exempt from licensing, including through non-conventional sources. Open access is allowed for transmission and distribution.

The Power Generation Policy of 2009 stated, "The consumption of electrical energy is a universal indicator of economic progress and well being of the people of any State. The per capita electricity consumption in Gujarat is almost twice the national average and is likely to increase further in the coming years. The capacity addition to meet the growing energy demand is expected to be both in public sector as well as private sector...At present, the share of private sector in total installed generation capacity is almost 25%.[8] Also, the State government supports greater competition in the sector through open access, intra-State ABT[9] etc."[10] There were also separate solar and wind power policies in 2009. At the end of 2010-11, GUVNL's Annual Report for 2010-11 shows an installed power generation capacity of 13,134 MW through conventional sources.[11] Of this, 60.7 per cent was thermal and 29.1 per cent was gas-based, nuclear and hydro accounting for the remainder.

---

7. *http://www.gidb.org/downloads/vol_1B_summary_2020.pdf*

8. However, the share of the private sector in total installed generation capacity is now 40%, not 25%.

9. Availability-based tariff.

10. *http://www.gseb.com/guvnl/PDFFiles%5CPower_policy2009.pdf*

11. *http://www.gseb.com/DownloadFiles/File/GUVNL/Annual_report_201011-12-1.pdf*

**Table 4.2**

*Installed Capacity: Conventional, 31st March 2012*

| Sr. No. | Name of Power Station | Fuel | Derated Capacity in MW |
|---|---|---|---|
| | GSECL | | |
| 1 | Dhuwaran TPS | Gas | 219 |
| 2 | Ukai TPS | Coal | 850 |
| 3 | Wanakbori TPS | Coal | 1470 |
| 4 | Gandhinagar TPS | Coal | 870 |
| 5 | Sikka TPS | Coal | 240 |
| 6 | Kachchh Lignite TPS | Lignite | 290 |
| 7 | Utran STG-l | Gas | 135 |
| 8 | Utran STG-ll | Gas | 374.5 |
| 9 | Kadana Hydro | Hydro | 240 |
| 10 | Ukai Hydro | Hydro | 300 |
| 11 | Ukai LB Hydro | Hydro | 5 |
| 12 | Panam Hydro | Hydro | 2 |
| | | Sub Total : | 4995.5 |
| | IPP | | |
| 1 | A.E.CO./Torrent | Coal/Gas | 500 |
| 2 | GIPCL–Vadodara | Gas/Naphtha | 310 |
| 3 | Sugen | Gas | 1147.5 |
| 4 | GIPCL–Mangrol | Lignite | 500 |
| 5 | Essar Power | Gas | 300 |
| 6 | Essar Power | Coal | 500 |
| 7 | GPEC–Paguthan | Gas | 655 |
| 8 | GSEGL–Hazira | Gas | 507 |
| 9 | GMDC Stage I | Lignite | 250 |
| | | Sub Total : | 4669.5 |
| | Central Sector (Gujarat's Share) | | |
| 1 | NPC-Tarapur APC & TAPP #4 | Nuclear | 434 |
| 2 | NPC-Kakrapar APC | Nuclear | 125 |
| 3 | NTPC Corba | Coal | 456 |
| 4 | NTPC Vindhyachal -1 | Coal | 230 |
| 5 | NTPC Vindhyachal -2 | Coal | 239 |
| 6 | NTPC Vindhyachal -3 | Coal | 266 |
| 7 | NTPC Kawas | Gas | 187 |
| 8 | NTPC Zanor | Gas | 237 |
| 9 | SIPAT | Coal | 633 |
| 10 | KAHALGAON | Coal | 141 |
| | | Sub Total : | 2948 |
| 1 | Sardar Sarovar–SSNNL | Hydro | 232 |
| | Bilateral | | |
| 1 | Adani Power Limited | Coal | 2000 |
| 2 | A.C.B. (India) Ltd | Coal | 100 |
| 3 | UMPP Mundra CGPL | Coal | 361 |
| | | Sub Total : | 2461 |
| | | Total : | 15306 |

However, these are slightly dated figures and around 6,000 MW more is in the pipeline. For conventional power, Table 4.2 shows a more current figure of installed capacity, as of 31st March 2012.[12] For 2010-11, those somewhat dated figures, show a non-conventional installed capacity of 2,116 MW, almost 99 per cent accounted for by wind. CEA (Central Electricity Authority) has more current figures and for July 2012, gives a total (including non-conventional) installed capacity of 23,927 MW, 6,286 from state-owned entities, 14,249 MW from private entities and 3,392 MW from central utilities.[13] Non-conventional energy has benefitted from fiscal incentives incorporated in the policies.

In 2001, Gujarat was a power deficit state, by roughly around 2,000 MW. By the end of 2012, Gujarat will have a power surplus of around 2,000 MW, though expected increases in GSDP growth also increase the demand for power. However, the Gujarat success story is not just about the macro generation situation. It is also about reduction in T&D (transmission and distribution) losses, down from 35.90 per cent in 2002-03 to 22.20 per cent in 2006-07.[14] It is 20.13 per cent in 2010-11. This is partly because T&D losses are not actually T&D losses. They are also about theft and unmetered supply. Other than metering, theft of electricity became a criminal offence and the law

12. *http://guj-epd.gov.in/epd_projects.htm.*

13. *http://cea.nic.in/reports/monthly/inst_capacity/jul12.pdf*

14. Chaudhury, P.R. (n.d.). *Reforms and Loss Reduction Strategies – Gujarat Experience. http://ugvcl.info/presentation/prchoudhary.pdf.*

was enforced, with distributors insulated from political pressures. This last factor is rarely mentioned, but has been an important one, across all of Gujarat's various reform experiments. There were special checking squads for checking installation, especially for HT (high-tech) connections, and ex-army personnel were roped in. In Sabarmati, Surat, Rajkot, Bhavnagar and Baroda, there were special police stations for power theft. Provisions were made for sealed meters that were tamper-proof. Through an e-Urja project, electronic billing and payment was introduced. Faulty meters were replaced. Unauthorised connections were regularised through one-time settlements.

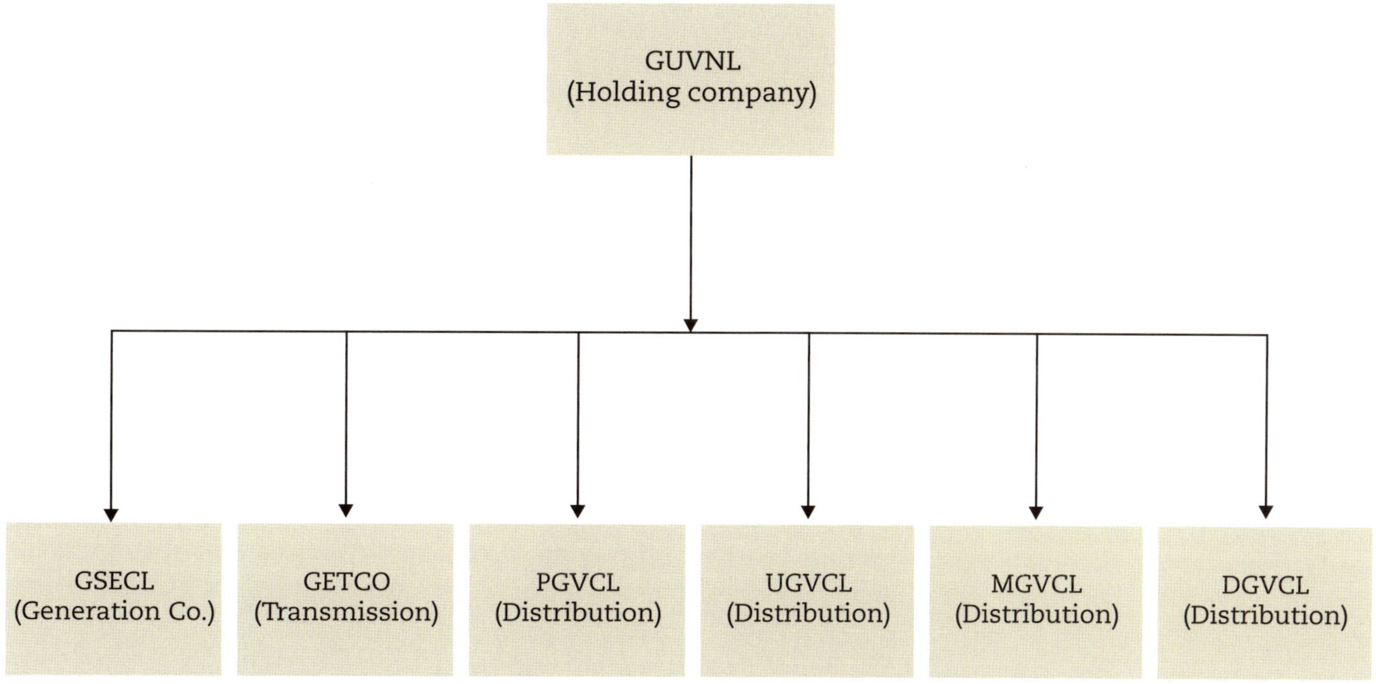


Having said this, T&D losses of 20.13 per cent are still high. They ought not to be in excess of 10 per cent or thereabouts, even lower. This is largely explained by significant intrastate variation. For example, in Gandhinagar and Surat, where Torrent Power Limited handles the distribution, T&D losses are 6.84 per cent. So far, the focus on reducing T&D losses has been in some geographical segments and areas, not everywhere. One must also remember that reduction in T&D losses are also a function of investing in transmission equipment.

Understandably, these power sector reforms have received awards and the box shows awards received in 2010 and 2011.[15] However, the power sector

15. Information collated from GUVNL's annual report, *http://www.gseb.com/DownloadFiles/File/GUVNL/Annual_report_201011-12-1.pdf*

**Box 4.1**

*Power Sector Awards*

State Power Utility Award, Indian Chamber of Commerce, Kolkata

Enertia Award for investment-friendly state in energy and power, Falcon Media,

Tech Excellence Award for e-Urja, India Tech Foundation, Mumbai

Power India Excellence Award, India Tech Foundation

Overall distribution utility performance award to MGVCL for DRUM project in Umreth, Council for Power Utility, New Delhi

Indi Power Award to UGVCL for energy efficiency, conservation and demand-side management, Council for Power Utility, New Delhi

Infrastructure Today KPMG Award to GUVNL

Excellence in cost management award to PGVCL, Institute of Costs and Works Accountants of India

reform story is not just about this, which brings us to the JGY (Jyotigram Yojana) project. JGY ensures 3-phase power supply to all villages. The 2001 Census showed that Gujarat had 18,066 villages. It was impossible to electrify 35 of these. They were submerged in projects connected with dams, had no populations and were uninhabited, or were located in remote, dense and reserved forest areas. All the others were meant to be electrified. As a pilot project, JGY was launched in 2003 and was completed in 2006. Other than the 18,066 villages, 9,700 hamlets around those villages were also covered. The key was a bifurcation of supply lines into dedicated agricultural feeders. For agricultural use, one would thus be ensured continuous power for eight hours a day, at predetermined times. For other rural loads (domestic, commercial and industrial), there would be 24/7 power. 24/7, 3-phase supply was provided to JGY feeders. These then provided 8 hours of 3-phase continuous supply to agricultural feeders and 1-phase 24/7 power to other rural uses. The argument about people wanting subsidised power and refusing to pay higher tariffs is misplaced. People are prepared to pay, provided that the quality of power supply improves. It was no different for JGY. Once power at predetermined hours was available, there was less of an incentive to divert subsidised power for agriculture to domestic household use. But JGY also had to be tweaked a bit. There were consumers who actually lived on farms and they were ignored in the process of bifurcation. GUVNL then devised special transformers that could provide electricity to such consumers, both for domestic and commercial use. In the course of JGY, 56,307 km of HT lines, 22,146 km of LT (low-tech) lines and 18,724 transformers were set up. JGY helped reduce T&D losses. It also helped reduce transformer failures. More importantly, it led to all villages being electrified, without load shedding, and this had positive socio-economic multiplier benefits.

This is what the Planning Commission had to say on JGY.[16] "A major factor contributing to a rapid fall in water tables in India is the availability of free or cheap power. Now the latter has also become a consequence of the former, as farmers need power to reach lower depths to extract groundwater. Complete elimination of power subsidies would have a major negative impact on farm livelihoods. But there is a way out as shown especially by the *Jyotigram* scheme in Gujarat. Feeders supplying power to tube wells are separated from other rural feeders. Now villages get full day three-phase power for domestic use, schools, hospitals, and village industries. Farmers get eight hours of full-voltage three-phase power according to a pre-announced schedule. Predictable, reliable, high-quality, even if rationed power, appears a better deal for farmers than the earlier erratic, poor quality supply that incentivized stolen power. This has made possible real-time co-management of electricity and groundwater of which there are few other examples across the globe." A 2005 study by Confederation of Indian Industry (CII) and the IRMA (Institute of Rural Management) found the following benefits from JGY[17]—Employment increased; out-migration from rural Gujarat declined by 33 per cent; drop-outs of girl children from schools declined by 80 per cent; school absenteeism went down by 13 per cent; the average duration of study at home increased by 92 per cent for girls and 81 per cent for boys; rural women spent 90 per cent more time on education, 88 per cent more time on entertainment, 43 per cent more time on social activities, 18 per cent more time on income generation activities; rural women spent 26 per cent less time on household chores; 53 per cent of families in rural areas could now work at night on rural industries; and activities like diamond polishing, toiletries and agro processing received a boost. There is a paper on Gujarat's agricultural performance that is often quoted.[18] We will talk about the agricultural performance in a subsequent chapter. For the moment, that paper said, "Rationing of farm power supply post-Jyotigram brought about a certain order and discipline in the extraction of groundwater, but the improved quality and reliability of farm power supply also made it possible

16. *Mid-Term Appraisal of the Eleventh Five Year Plan, 2010, http://planningcommission.nic.in/plans/mta/11th_mta/chapterwise/Comp_mta11th.pdf*

17. *http://www.gujaratcmfellowship.org/document/Gujarat%20Overall%20Development/Jyotigram%20Yojana%20Article_Devika%20Devaiah_2010.pdf*

18. Shah, Tushaar, Ashok Gulati, P. Hemant, Ganga Shreedhar and R.C. Jain (2009). "Secret of Gujarat's Agrarian Miracle after 2000," *Economic and Political Weekly* 52. *http://www.gujaratcmfellowship.org/document/Agriculture/Secret%20of%20Gujarat%20Agrarian%20Miracle_EPW_26Dec09.pdf*

for farmers to make ambitious plans to grow Bt cotton and wheat on a large scale."

Therefore, in addition to other power sector awards, it is understandable that JGY should receive specific awards, the latest being one by the Stockholm International Water Institute. But JGY has received several other awards too. Though we will return to such issues later, before moving on from the power sector, one should mention that there are other power sector schemes too, catering to specific deprived segments. There is the Kutir Jyoti scheme, which provides single-point free lighting connections to BPL (below poverty line) families in tribal districts. There is the Zupada Vijlikaran scheme, which mirrors this for general category BPL families. And there is the Central RGGVY (Rajiv Gandhi Grameen Vidyutikaran Yojana).

If power is important to better people's lives, water is no less so. There are several dimensions to water and we will focus on some of these in later chapters. In this chapter, one is only interested in the aggregate or overall picture. The overall picture is that Gujarat is a water scarce state. On an average, the availability of fresh water is 1,137 cubic metres per person per annum. This is way below the all-India average of 2,000 cubic metres. Region-wise, it is even more serious, since south and central Gujarat is the only part of the state where there is relatively abundant supply of water. Even there, the average availability for south and central Gujarat is below the national average, with the exception of the limited geographical area of the Dangs. Kachchh has water, but much of that is saline. In neighbouring areas, this has led to the degradation of groundwater. Saurashtra is deficient in water and the worst affected is north Gujarat. If the per capita per annum availability of water is less than 1,700 cubic meters, a region is 'water stressed'. And if the figure is less than 1,000 cubic meters, a region is 'water scarce'. To place matters in perspective, the figures are 540 for Saurashtra, 343 for north Gujarat and 719 for Kachchh. Making matters worse, subsidised power to farmers and absence of regulation on groundwater has historically led to groundwater depletion. The only three perennial rivers are Narmada, Tapi and Mahi, all three of which flow through south Gujarat. Sabarmati is a non-perennial river and flows through Sabarkantha, Mehsana and Ahmedabad. Rainfall is erratic and the state has therefore been subject to droughts.

With this background, there are several strands in the water sector reforms—inter-basin transfer of water from surplus areas to deficit areas like north Gujarat, Saurashtra and Kachchh; the linking of canals; water conservation; participatory irrigation management; micro-irrigation; check dams and smaller dams (such as through the Sardar Patel Water Conservation Programme); deepening of ponds; cleaning and restoration of step wells; community management of water supply in villages through WASMO (Water

**Table 4.3**

*Institutional Structure of Water Sector*

| *Agency* | *Jurisdiction* | *Role* |
|---|---|---|
| Department of Narmada, Water Resources and Water Supplies | State | Regulation and oversight of sector, oversight of state government corporations involved in water schemes |
| Department of Urban Development | State | Oversight and regulation of urban local bodies, excluding corporations |
| Municipal corporations | Major cities | Retail water supply |
| Municipalities and Nagar Palikas | Smaller cities | Retail water supply |
| *Gram panchayats* | Villages | Retail water supply |
| Gujarat Industrial Development Corporation (GIDC) | State | Retail water supply in industrial estates |
| Gujarat Water Supply and Sewerage Board (GWSSB) | State | Mostly urban water supply and sewerage |
| Gujarat State Drinking Water Company Limited | State | Bulk transmission and supply of drinking water |
| Sardar Sarovar Narmada Nigam Limited | State | Wholesale water supply |

and Sanitation Management Organisation); and the SSY (Sujalam Suphalam Yojana). Water has both a drinking water and an irrigation water component. Something like SSY covers both. While irrigation water belongs to a slightly different category, the management and institutional structure for drinking water is that shown in Table 4.3.[19]

While the state has certainly gained because of Sardar Sarovar, that would not have been possible without the state-wide water supply grid. This involves inter-basin transfer of water and intends to provide drinking water to 14,305 villages and 171 towns (roughly 75% of the population) through bulk water transmission pipelines, water treatment plants, service reservoirs and distribution pipeline networks. But perhaps one ought to step back a bit. Rural water supply through the ARWSP (Accelerated Rural Water Supply Programme) is a central government Bharat Nirman scheme and Gujarat covered several habitations through this. In addition, the Swajaldhara rural drinking water scheme was launched as a central project in 2002. Gujarat implements this through WASMO. Through WASMO, *pani samitis* have been

19. *http://www.gidb.org/gidb/cms.aspx?content_id=204*

formed and these work through PRIs (panchayti raj institutions) and NGOs (non-governmental organisations). While there will be more on WASMO later, it is early days yet. The geographical coverage is still limited and user fees, where imposed, do not lead to complete cost recovery. This is equally true of water taxes in urban areas. In addition to the central government schemes, the state-water supply grid was an important and extremely significant supplement. In addition to the Sardar Sarovar-based drinking water supply project and the afore-mentioned SSY, this has several (around 450) regional schemes. There is also a separate Kalpasar freshwater reservoir project.

Figure 4.1 shows the state-wide drinking water supply grid. While all of it has not been completed, it covers around 36.2 million of the population already. Therefore, the percentage of households that have tap connections has increased from 26.6 per cent in 2002 to 72.22 per cent in 2011. There has

**Figure 4.1**

*State-wide Drinking Water Supply Grid*

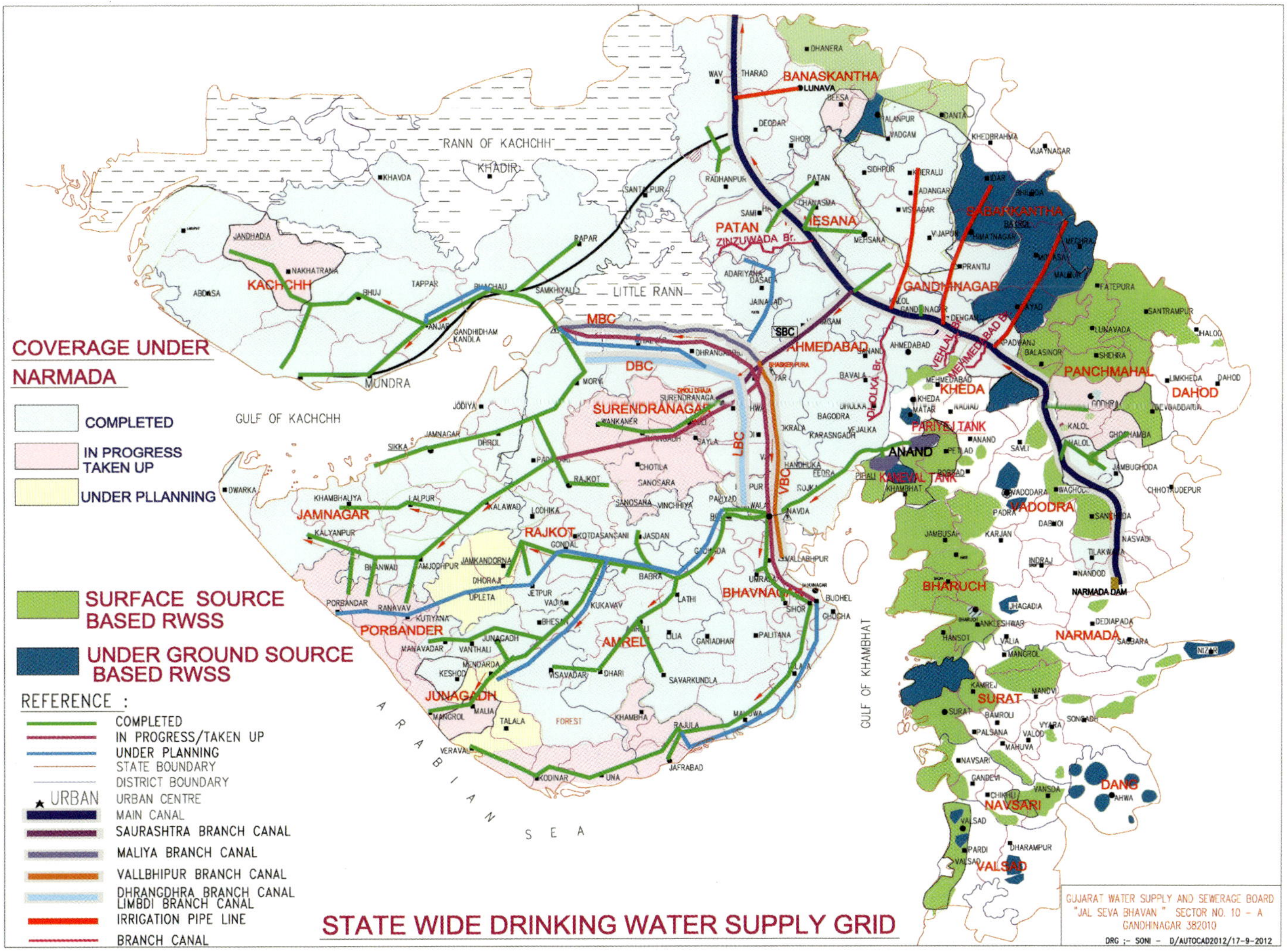

been a sharp fall in the number of deep tube wells from 1,146 in 2000-01 to 47 in 2008-09. In 2001, 4,054 villages were supplied water through tankers. In 2010, that number dropped to 210.

Irrigation water is somewhat different, though something like SSY covers both drinking and irrigation water. For the present, it is enough to note that the Sardar Sarovar project has also assured irrigation to several parts of Gujarat, in particular districts like Narmada, Bharuch, Vadodara, Panchmahal, Kheda, Anand, Ahmedabad, Gandhinagar, Mehsana, Patan, Banaskantha, Surendranagar, Bhavnagar, Rajkot and Kachchh. Large chunks of the Sardar Sarovar project have still not been completed. However, when we look at agriculture, we will find that improved access to irrigation, in addition to access to power, has already transformed the nature of Gujarat's agriculture.

In terms of affecting people's lives for the better, roads are just as important as electricity and water. Compared to many other states, Gujarat has always had relatively better road infrastructure. 98.27 per cent of state highways and 96.93 per cent of major district roads possess asphalt surfaces. 85.63 per cent of other district roads and village roads also possess asphalt surfaces. 98.84 per cent of villages are connected by '*pucca*' roads. Gujarat has also benefitted from NHDP (National Highway Development Project). Given the base, the focus has thus been more on upgradation and maintenance, improving access in relatively disadvantaged regions, while simultaneously tapping the proposed DFC (Dedicated Freight Corridor) between Delhi and Mumbai and the DMIC (Delhi-Mumbai Industrial Corridor). In so far as relatively disadvantaged regions are concerned, the emphasis has been on all-weather connectivity, particularly in coastal, tribal and border areas. There have been several PPP projects, sometimes externally-aided, with provisions for tolls. The Gujarat Highways Bill of 2007 facilitated PPP (public private partnership) projects. There is also a Pragati Path Yojana, for improvement of state highways, part of which has been completed. In addition, for major projects, third party inspection and monitoring has been introduced. Maintenance guarantees of 3 to 5 years are incorporated in contracts. IT tools have been used for physical monitoring, registration of contractors, court cases and departmental enquiries. In high rainfall districts like Navasari and Surat, village roads have been constructed with cement/concrete.

Towards the beginning of this chapter, several physical infrastructure areas were listed out. Of these, *bijli*, *pani* and *sadak* are the most important and in this chapter, we have argued that all three have improved in Gujarat, transforming people's lives. A part of this has been fortuitous, but the rest of it has been by design. For example, in addition to the standard template

Figure 4.2

*Irrigation Map of Gujarat*

| Status | Major | Medium | StateMinor | Total |
|---|---|---|---|---|
| Completed | 18 | 87 | 118 | 223 |
| Ongoing | SS (N) P | 10 | 26 | 36 +SS(N )P |
| Under Tendering Stage | 5 | 13 | 17 | 35 |
| Under Investi-Stage | 2 | 25 | 99 | 126 |
| Total | 25+SS(N)P | 135 | 260 | 420+SS(N)P |

of electricity sector reforms, JGY was an extremely novel and successful reform initiative. In the water sector, while Gujarat benefitted from Sardar Sarovar, those benefits would have been limited had it not been for the state-wide water distribution grid. Roads are slightly different, since in this sector, Gujarat has clearly benefitted from initiatives that were exogenous to the state, NHDP, DFC and DMIC being examples of that.

For the sake of completeness, one should now talk about the other physical infrastructure sectors that we have ignored. We will turn to those in Chapter 5.

**Figure 4.3**

*Pragatipath Yojana*

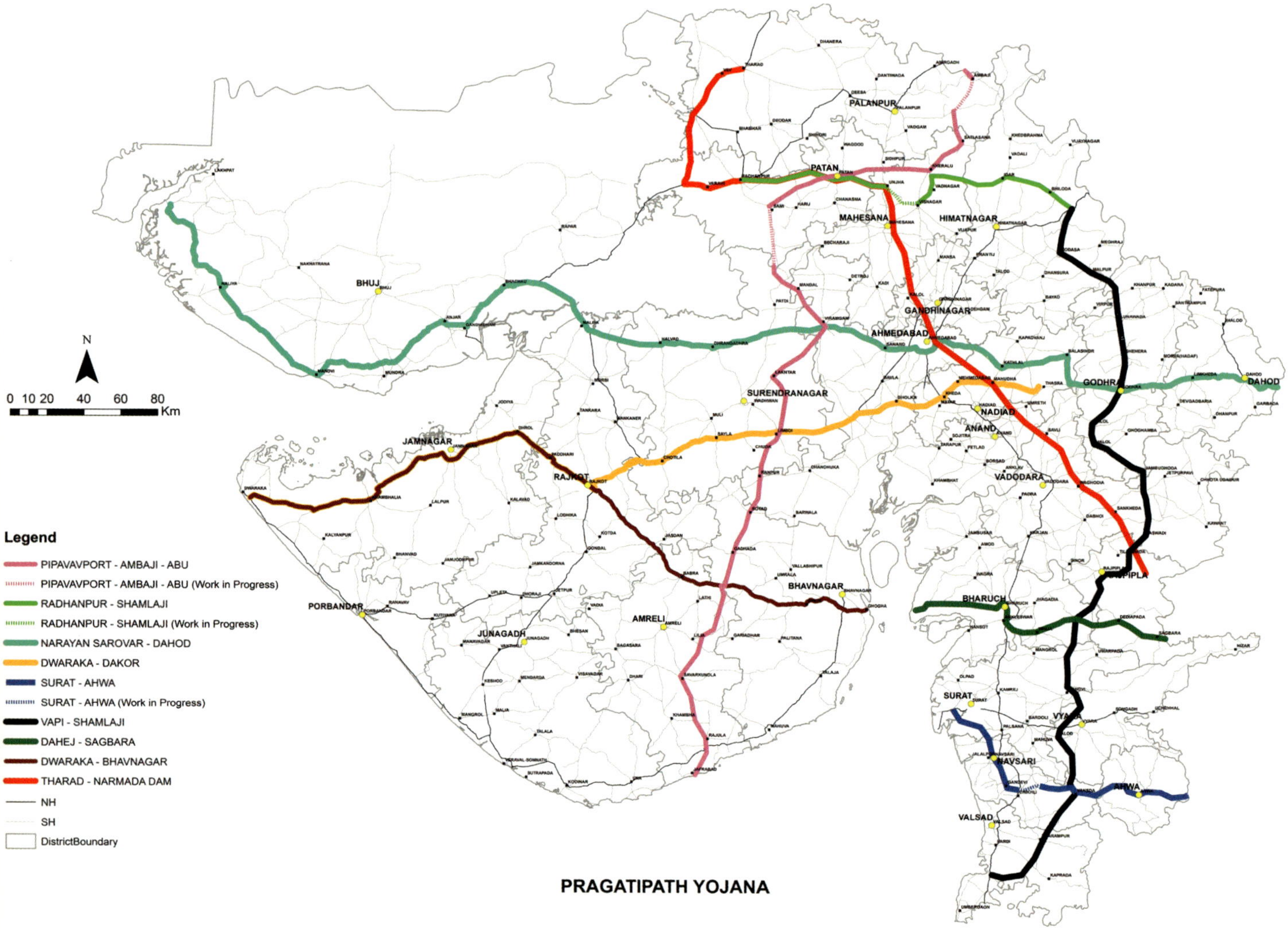

Pragatipath Yojana
Mehsana Vishanagar Kheralu Ambaji road
Km 26/00 -27/00

# 5

# The Other Elements of Physical Infrastructure

LET US GO BACK to the listing of physical infrastructure mentioned in the BIG-2020 report.[1] To recapitulate these were—(1) ports; (2) power; (3) roads; (4) railways; (5) aviation; (6) urban infrastructure; (7) urban transport; (8) water supply; (9) industrial parks; (10) information technology; (11) gas; and (12) tourism. Out of these, we talked about power, roads and water supply in Chapter 4. Though one does not necessarily have to agree with this perception, power, roads and water supply can be described as inclusive. The others are more elitist, they cater to specific segments, like industry or urban areas. At least, that can be a perception though there are poor people also in urban areas.

According to the 2001 Census, 37.3 per cent of Gujarat's population is urban. Across states, this is high and this is understandable. Globally, economic development has been correlated with urbanisation. There are several reasons why villages disappear. Thanks to migration and improved connectivity, some disappear. Others become mainstreamed into urban agglomerations. Still others are reclassified as urban, as development proceeds. All these are desirable developments. Economically, urban areas provide efficiencies in production, marketing and distribution and even in labour and job markets. There are three kinds of resistance articulated against a rural to urban transition. The first is a sentimental kind of association with some notion of a rural Arcadia, even if this ideal does not actually exist. The second kind of argument is based on the premise that with this transition, there will be a food security problem. This fails to appreciate the low productivity levels Indian agriculture possesses, not only in comparisons with the rest of the world, but also in comparisons between India's irrigated and non-irrigated areas. The third argument is directed against the kind of urban life that is delivered, with pressures on urban infrastructure like water supply, sewage clearance and drainage, waste disposal, transportation, power, housing, law and order and environmental pollution issues, not to speak of slums. This is less an argument against urbanisation and is more of an argument against the kind of urbanisation that takes place. For purposes of the present chapter, the relevant argument is only the third one. Since Gujarat is a rapidly growing state, it will also rapidly urbanise and by 2020, almost 50 per cent of the state's population may be urban and this includes residents in new townships.

Compared to some other states, Gujarat does possess a relative advantage, in the sense that there is no single large city that is the dominant magnet. While there is certainly a difference between an urban area and its extended urban agglomeration, there is a broad base of eight cities with municipal corporations—Ahmedabad, Gandhinagar, Vadodara, Surat, Rajkot, Jamnagar,

1. *http://www.gidb.org/downloads/vol_1B_summary_2020.pdf*

ખેતી-ખેડૂત-ગામડાની
સમૃદ્ધિની યોજના
"કિસાન પથ"

મોટીદાઉ - 2 - K.M.
ઊંઝા
મહેસાણા.

Junagadh and Bhavnagar. While trends cannot necessarily be extrapolated, 60 per cent of the present urban population is in these seven cities with municipal corporations. There are other smaller cities with municipalities—Class I (more than 100,000 population, barring the ones with municipal corporations), Class II (between 50,001 and 100,000) and Classes III and IV (less than 50,000). Eighty-five (85) per cent of the urban population is accounted for by Classes I and II (including the ones with municipal corporations). In other words, if one takes care of these urban areas and caters to urban services for these residents, a large chunk of urban infrastructure will be taken care of.

Ever since the Zakaria Committee in 1963, physical norms have been suggested for basic urban services like water supply (piped and potable), sanitation/sewerage, solid waste collection and disposal, storm water drains, housing, urban roads and public transport, street lighting and water for industrial and commercial use.[2] There have also been attempts to convert these into monetary estimates of cost of delivery, though these vary, depending on the type of urban centre. These do not concern us now, except to note that the monetary costs are considerable, despite economies of scale in service delivery and possibilities of self-generation of funds. After the 74th Constitutional Amendment, most of the urban services mentioned above become the responsibility of urban bodies. For some of these urban

**Table 5.1**

*Status of Core Infrastructure in ULBs*

| | *Corporations* | *Class I Municipalities* | *Class II Municipalities* | *Class III Municipalities* | *Class IV Municipalities* |
|---|---|---|---|---|---|
| Network coverage of sewerage and drainage | Available, inadequate | Available, inadequate | Grossly inadequate or not available | Grossly inadequate or unavailable | Grossly inadequate or unavailable |
| Treatment facilities for sewerage | Adequate | Available, inadequate | Grossly inadequate or not available | Grossly inadequate or unavailable | Grossly inadequate or unavailable |
| Collection and transportation solid waste | Adequate | Available, inadequate | Available, inadequate | Available, inadequate | Grossly inadequate of or unavailable |
| Waste treatment and disposal | Adequate in some, inadequate in others | Grossly inadequate or unavailable | Grossly inadequate or unavailable | Grossly inadequate or unavailable | Grossly inadequate or unavailable |
| Density of paved roads | Adequate | Adequate | Adequate | Adequate | Available, inadequate |
| Public transport | Inadequate in general | Grossly inadequate or unavailable | Grossly inadequate or unavailable | Grossly inadequate or unavailable | Grossly inadequate or unavailable |

2. See, Mathur, M.P., Rajesh Chandra, Satpal Singh and Basudha Chattopadhyaya (2007). "Norms and Standards of Municipal Basic Services in India", National Institute of Urban Affairs *Working Paper*, April. *http://www.niua.org/Publications/working_papers/N&S%20 working%20paper.pdf*

services, Table 5.1, based on the BIG report,[3] shows the present status. The broad picture is that there is a continuum of deterioration. One is relatively better off in corporations and Class I and II municipalities, but considerably worse off in Class III and IV municipalities. Greenfield cities and towns are always easier to plan for, be they in SIRs (special investment regions), SEZs (special economic zones), greenfield ports and SIRs (special industrial areas) along the DFC (dedicated freight corridors) and DMIC (Delhi-Mumbai industrial corridors), or away from them, or special industrial regions like Dholera, or GIFT (Gujarat International Finance Tec-City).

Table 5.2 shows that several municipal corporations in Gujarat have won awards in assorted sectors. But there are a few questions one needs to ask. First, urban infrastructure cannot be only for greenfield projects or corporations and Class I and II municipalities. What happens to Class III and IV municipalities? Second, there is an issue of municipal finances. The relevant statutory provisions are the Bombay Provincial Municipal Corporation Act of 1949 and the Gujarat Municipalities Act of 1963. Under the Gujarat Town Planning and Urban Development Act of 1976, there are separate urban development authorities too. These various pieces of legislation allow the levying of relevant taxes. Other than motor vehicles, the major one has to be property taxes. While corporations have been successful in raising revenue through such taxes, and even in raising municipal bonds, that is not an argument that can yet be advanced for Class III and IV municipalities. Nor has there been a great deal of success in imposing the right user charges for municipal services, or raising revenue through municipal undertakings, the increases still falling short of what is required. Therefore, finances are sustained through grants-in-aid. Third, it is not just about revenue. There is also the matter of urban land and freeing up surplus land for development, including development by the private sector. The Urban Land (Ceiling and Regulation) Act of 1976 no longer exists. It was repealed in 1999, but has not been replaced by an alternative piece of legislation. Consequently,

**Table 5.2**

*Awards Received by Municipal Corporations*

| *Municipal Corporation* | *Year* | *Sector* |
|---|---|---|
| Ahmedabad | 2012 | Best practices |
| Ahmedabad | 2011 | Urban poor |
| Surat | 2011 | Urban governance |
| Rajkot | 2011 | e-governance |
| Ahmedabad | 2010 | Urban poor |
| Ahmedabad | 2010 | Transport |
| Surat | 2009 | Energy conservation |
| Surat | 2009 | Urban poor |
| Surat | 2009 | Financial management |
| Surat | 2009 | Urban governance |
| Surat | 2009 | Power generation |
| Surat | 2009 | Water supply |
| Ahmedabad | 2009 | Transport, mass transit |
| Surat | 2008-09 | Urban transport |
| Surat | 2008-09 | Public transport |
| Vadodara | 2008 | Energy conservation |
| Vadodara | 2008 | Public transportation |
| Ahmedabad | 2008 | e-governance |
| Surat | 2007-08 | e-governance |
| Surat | 2007-08 | Urban transport |
| Jamnagar | 2006-07 | Water supply |
| Ahmedabad | 2006-07 | Urban poor |

3. *op.cit.* no. 1.

clearances are still formally required. It is not quite obvious why an alternative piece of legislation, that moves clearances from the executive to the statutory, has not yet been mooted. Fourth, other than finance, there is also an issue of capacity and human resources within municipalities and there is a bit of problem in the smaller ones. Fifth, 'urban' and 'rural' have census definitions. Accordingly, above a threshold, a municipality is formed and depending on some criteria, there is a *panchayat*. There is a hinterland between PRIs (Panchayati Raj Institutions) and municipalities, where because of rapid development and urbanisation, a village is reclassified as urban. In that hinterland, there seems to be a governance problem in the interim, where the capacities of a municipality, or that of a PRI, are both non-existent. The RURBAN idea is meant to address this.

However, the issue is not just warts and blemishes, as they stand. It should be more about what is being done to rectify the situation. One gets a sense from the GUDM (Gujarat Urban Development Mission), which was set up in 2006 as a nodal agency for the JNNURM (Jawaharlal Nehru National Urban Renewal Mission), but has a mandate that extends beyond it now. Other than JNNURM, there are central schemes like UIG (Urban Infrastructure and Governance), BSUP (Basic Services to the Urban Poor), UIDSSMT (Urban Infrastructure Development Scheme for Small and Medium Towns), IHSDP (Integrated Housing and Slum Development Programme) and RAY (Rajiv Awas Yojana). A point was made earlier about Gujarat's ability to plug gaps in central schemes with state-level ones. In the present context, the relevant ones are the GSY (Garib Samruddhi Yojana) and the SJMMSVY (Swarnim Jayanti Mukhya Mantri Shaheri Vikas Yojana). SJMMSVY is an important one to flag, because it plugs a gap. Most taxes are paid by urban residents, but almost all flagship schemes are meant for rural areas. While JNNURM is an exception, JNNURM is restricted to the upper tier of urban India. In contrast, SJMMSVY covers 159 towns, apart from the 8 municipalities. The MSWMP (Municipal Solid Waste Management Project) should also be mentioned. UMEED is slightly different, since it is more of a skill upgradation programme for urban youth.

With regulations for rehabilitation and redevelopment of slums passed in 2010, one should also mention the slums. Census data do not cover slum populations for all cities. Broadly speaking, an aggregate figure would be something like 23 per cent of India's urban population living in slums, with far higher figures in some metros. Since Gujarat's urban population is more evenly distributed and there is not quite a metro, though Ahmedabad approaches that, Gujarat's slum figures are marginally lower than that all-India average. But slums do exist, at just about 20 per cent of the urban population, such in cities like Surat, Ahmedabad and Vadodara. What is been the impact of schemes like GSY or SJMMSVY? Outside the corporations and

Class I and II municipalities, that is a tough one to answer. One does have figures on expenditure, even on the construction of houses for slum-dwellers and the involvement of *sakhi mandals* and SHGs (self help groups) in MSWMP. One also knows that DUDAs (District Urban Development Agencies) have been restructured and strengthened, a common cadre has been created for ULBs (urban local bodies), socio-economic surveys are being conducted for BPL (below poverty line) families with the intention of using biometric cards and that there will be policies on slum-dwellers and street-vendors. Having said this, since this focus essentially dates from 2005, it is a bit premature to gauge success, particularly for Class III and IV municipalities. However, the existence of a plan is an undeniable positive.

While on the subject of urban planning, or planning in general, it is odd that one of Gujarat's remarkable successes does not get written about that much, even in government publications. This is the use of GIS (geographic information system) maps in decision making. This is through the BISAG (Bhaskaracharya Institute for Space Applications and Geo-Informatics), a state-level nodal agency set up in 1997 and renamed BISAG in 2003. BISAG also conducts training programmes and workshops and is involved in delivering over the Gujarat Satcom (satellite communication) network. But more importantly, it uses remote sensing and GIS to facilitate planning. These GIS maps with several layers have already been introduced in all the municipalities and are being extended to all urban areas. Figure 5.1 illustrates

**Figure 5.1**

*Urban Information System*

the kind of use that can be made of such maps in urban planning.[4] Among other things, this is certainly one initiative that other states should replicate. While not relevant for present purposes, BISAG's revenue model is also an extremely interesting one.

Let us now move on to other areas of physical infrastructure. With the exception of IT and tourism, those elements of physical infrastructure mentioned earlier are integrated into the broader industrial policy. DFC and DMIC have already been mentioned. SIR (special investment region) Dholera and the Dahej PCPIR (petroleum chemical and petrochemical investment region) are like nodes that feed into this network, as are industrial nodes in Halol-Savli, Sanand, Santhalpur, Hazira, Becharji-Mandal and Kaligram-Maroli. That apart, there are industrial parks, industrial areas and SEZs, in addition to logistics parks in Ahmedabad, Bharuch, Palanpur-Mehsana and Gandhidham-Mundra.

**Figure 5.2**

*DMIC (Delhi-Mumbai Industrial Corridor) in Gujarat*

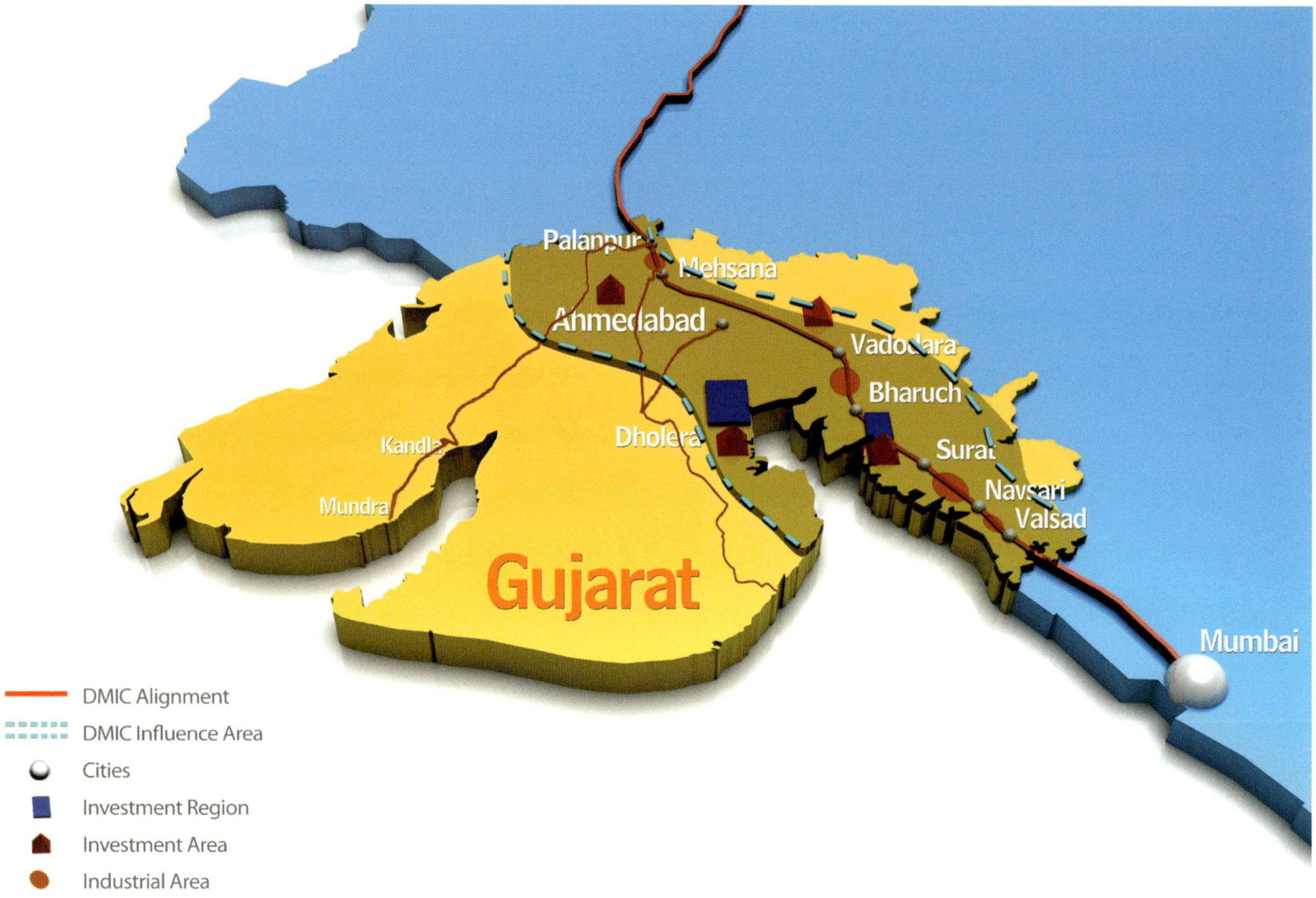


4. *http://www.bisag.gujarat.gov.in/urban.htm*

Gujarat was one of the first states to pass a SEZ Act, in 2004. Though there are several multi-product SEZs, most SEZs are in electronics/IT/ITES, followed by engineering. In any event, Gujarat was the first state which had an EPZ (export processing zone) in Kandla in 1965 and it was also a state which had the first private EPZ in Surat. There are several questions to ask in the context of a SEZ. At a time when import duties were high, and one could only liberalise in selected enclaves, there was obvious utility to something like a SEZ concept. But with import duties having declined in general, what is the utility of a SEZ? In part, the answer may lie in simplified procedures and better infrastructure. But in a general climate of liberalisation, such simplified procedures and better infrastructure should also be available everywhere, at least in principle. There can of course be a growth pole cum cluster formation kind of argument, linked to positive externalities generated from agglomeration. But that is not quite a SEZ argument either. One therefore suspects that the attractiveness of SEZs in Gujarat has quite a bit to do with the SEZ Act's provisions on the labour market. For example, there is easier exit, more flexible provisions on hiring and terminating labour and the concept of fixed term employment. There has been a conscious attempt to reduce the number of inspectors and self-certification has been introduced. Unlike other states, land acquisition has been less of a contentious issue in Gujarat, both for SEZs and in general. There are several reasons for this. Often wasteland and non-agricultural private land has been transferred. There has been quite a bit of private acquisition of land, with the state staying out of the acquisition process. At least, the state has stayed out of the acquisition process for new SEZs. There was land that was already acquired and this was transferred by the GIDC (Gujarat Industrial Development Corporation) to SEZs. Finally, the opposition to SEZs may be portrayed as a land acquisition problem. But often it is a skills problem, in the sense that those who lose land lack skills and therefore do not necessarily see employment opportunities in a new project. One can thus probably deduce that this has been less of a problem in Gujarat.

**Figure 5.3**

*Dedicated Freight Corridor (DFC)*

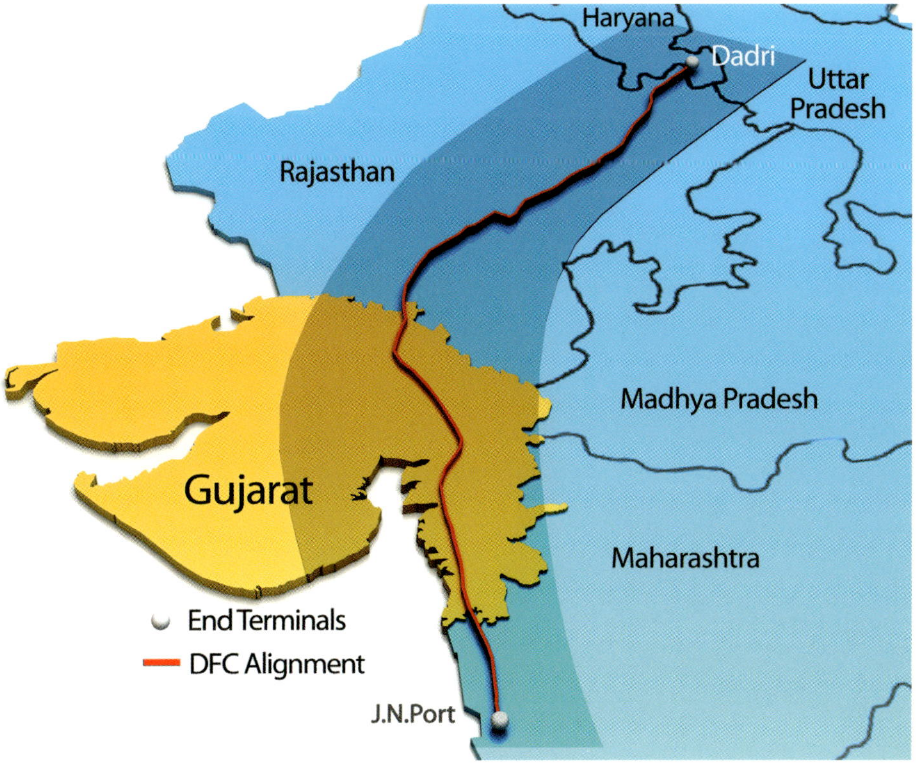

Other than SEZs, the 2009 Industrial Policy also provided for IRs (investment regions), SIRs (special investment regions) and IAs (industrial areas). Other than better physical connectivity, assured services and positive externalities through networks, the attractiveness clearly lies in simplified procedures, including those in the labour market. That apart, facilitation is provided in the land acquisition process. If there are SEZs, why have these regions? The answer has to do with the land acquisition process. In the case of a SEZ, the entire area will have to be acquired. However, for these, land acquisition in pockets is possible. There are road and rail connectivity projects that link these regions to DFC and DMIC areas. One should also mention airports. Other than improvement of air connectivity in existing airports and upgrading these, a new greenfield airport will be set up near Dholera SIR. These kinds of physical infrastructure improvements have led to industrial development and Gujarat's attractiveness as an investment destination. We will talk about this in a later chapter. However, the export success story requires a mention of seaports. Gujarat has a long coastline and major ports like Kandla, Diu and Daman are on the Union List of the Seventh Schedule. Therefore, what Gujarat has done with seaports is really a 'minor' ports story and it is also a private ports story. Given the year in which it was authored (1995), the

**Figure 5.4**

*Growth Centres and Industrial Estates of Gujarat*

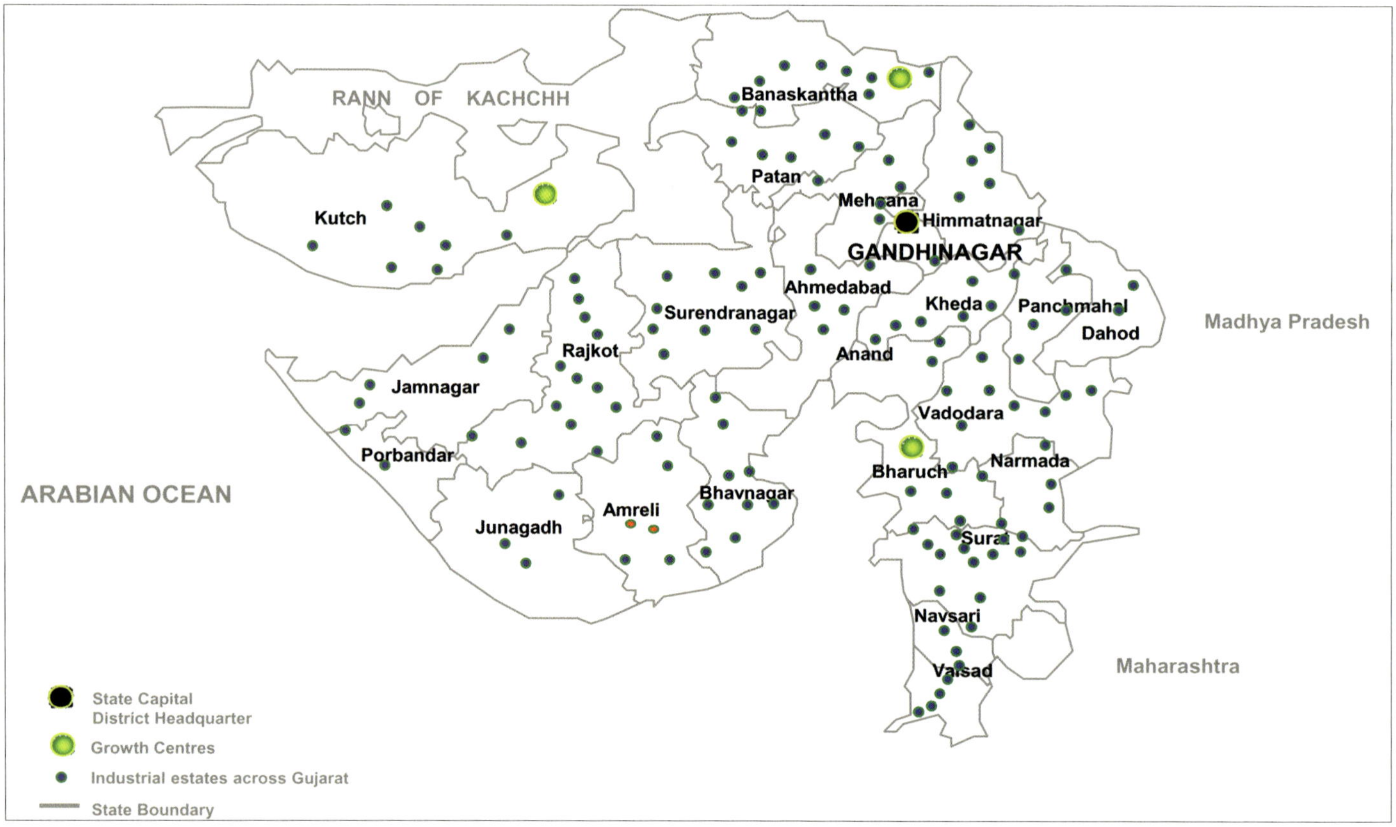

Port Policy was remarkably forward-looking and a long quote is necessary to illustrate how forward-looking it was.

"In 1991, Government of India initiated various economic, trade and industrial reforms, through the policy of liberalization to enhance industrial and trading activities. ...Gujarat State is one of those frontline States that can take up the policy of liberalization and privatization, announced by the Government of India through a process of globalization...Another major advantage is that, Gujarat has a vast hinterland consisting of fast developing Nothern and Central Indian States generating cargo. The States of Rajasthan, Madhya Pradesh, Western Uttar Pradesh, Delhi, Haryana, Punjab, Himachal Pradesh and Jammu & Kashmir, which constitute 35% of the total exports, are potential customers for Gujarat ports. Export of surplus foodgrains from these major grain producing States and import of fertilizers to these major consumers, offer great potential for growth of cargo in near future. Any economic development, taking place in these hinterland States have a direct bearing on Gujarat ports."[5] Of the 42 ports actually in Gujarat, Kandla is on the Union List. Ten (10) new sites were identified as direct berthing deepwater ports. While some ports would be developed by GMB (Gujarat Maritime Board), ports would also be built by the private sector. Captive jetties would be permitted for industries and some services (lighterage, dredging, piloting, tug-towing, essential utilities) would be privatised.

Thus, there are GMB ports. But there are also private ports on BOOT (build, own, operate, transfer) basis, to be transferred after 30 years. And there are several greenfield ports.

If one goes back to the list of physical infrastructure sectors, the only ones that are left are IT and tourism. There is nothing special to be said about either of these, except to mention that there are specific physical infrastructure projects targetted towards specific areas that are of tourism interest.

In the remainder of this chapter, let us therefore focus on something else, relevant because much of what Gujarat has accomplished in physical infrastructure represents a freeing up of space for the private sector, spliced with focussing public expenditure and improving its efficiency. While these points could have been made in subsequent chapters too, this is as good a place as any.

There exists a concept of economic freedom. While economic freedom is not the only kind of freedom that exists, there have been attempts to quantify and measure economic freedom, in a cross-country sense. EFW (*Economic Freedom of the World*) does this every year, as does the Index of Economic

5. *http://www.gmbports.org/downloads/port_policy_december_1995.pdf*

Freedom.[6] While economic freedom is difficult to pin down, quantify and measure, EFW now has a methodology based on five pillars—(1) size of government (expenditures, taxes and enterprises); (2) legal structure and security of property rights; (3) access to sound money; (4) freedom to trade internationally; and (5) regulation of credit, labour and business. Within these five components, there are sub-components. Cross-country, these kinds of studies show a strong correlation (depending on the context, positive or negative) between a country's score on EFW and assorted measures of economic development (life expectancy, percentage of children in the labour force, per capita income, average growth rate, income share of the poorest 10%, income level of the poorest 10%, per capita investment, adult literacy, infant mortality and so on). Admittedly, this is correlation and not causation. However, when the correlation is so strong, across development and deprivation indicators, it does suggest causation. But the point is not to get into EFW ratings, or discuss how India performs on such cross-country surveys. India is a large and heterogeneous country. Therefore, all-India measures tend to blur differences across states. One effect of post-1991 reforms has been to shift the focus of policy change, and policy hindrance, to the level of the states. Consequently, some states have reformed faster than others and some states have grown faster than others. Some states are economically freer than others. The EFW methodology has accordingly been modified and applied to Indian states, excluding areas that are under the Union government. Therefore, the heads covered are size of government, legal structure and security of property rights and regulation of labour and business.[7] These are then aggregated into an overall head. For details of the methodology and the variables used, one should refer to that study. For this present chapter, the relevant ranking is the one on regulation of labour and business and perhaps the overall ranking. We will revisit the other two heads in subsequent chapters.

**Figure 5.5**

*Location of Greenfield Ports*

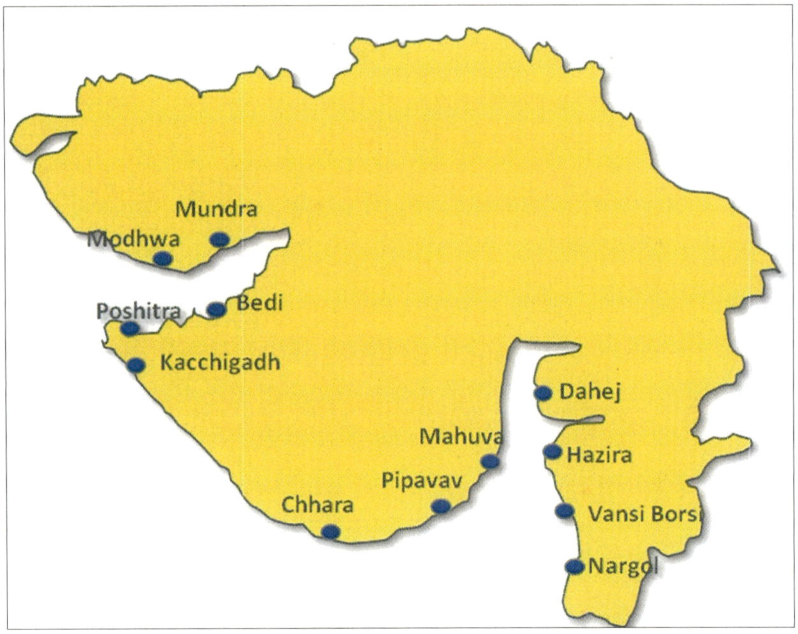


Table 5.3 shows what this study finds for the regulation of labour and business and Table 5.4 shows the overall rankings. Because of data limitations, the study only covers

6. *http://www.freedomhouse.org and http://www.heritage.org/index/default.*

7. Debroy, Bibek, Laveesh Bhandari, Ashok Gulati and Swaminathan Aiyar (2012). *The Economic Freedom Rankings for the States of India, 2012*. Cato Institute, Indicus Analytics, Friedrich Naumann Stiftung and Academic Foundation.

major states, not every state. Though this study was published in 2012, most data pertain to 2011.

Let us look at Table 5.3 first, which has both ranks and scores. One tends to focus on ranks, but the scores, which drive the ranks, are just as important. Indeed, it is the scores that determine the ranks. The higher the score, the better. Table 5.3 shows that on the regulation of labour and business, Gujarat has always been the best state and continues to be that in 2011 too. However, what is noticeable is the sharp improvement in Gujarat's scores since 2009. The overall rankings are influenced by the other two heads too. However, in the overall rankings too, Gujarat is the best state in 2011 and there is quite a bit of gap between Gujarat and the next state, Tamil Nadu. In addition, Gujarat's ranks and scores have improved over time and in the overall rankings, in 2011, Gujarat has dislodged Tamil Nadu, which had the no.1 slot in 2009. In the overall scores, Gujarat is now considerably ahead of Tamil Nadu.

**Table 5.3**

*Regulation of Labour and Business: State Ratings and Rankings*

| | *2005* | | *2009* | | *2011* | |
|---|---|---|---|---|---|---|
| *States* | *Score* | *Rank* | *Score* | *Rank* | *Score* | *Rank* |
| **Gujarat** | **0.47** | **1** | **0.49** | **1** | **0.67** | **1** |
| Himachal Pradesh | 0.36 | 7 | 0.38 | 5 | 0.63 | 2 |
| Jammu & Kashmir | 0.35 | 8 | 0.39 | 4 | 0.51 | 3 |
| Haryana | 0.32 | 11 | 0.34 | 7 | 0.47 | 4 |
| Andhra Pradesh | 0.33 | 10 | 0.48 | 2 | 0.45 | 5 |
| Madhya Pradesh | 0.46 | 3 | 0.27 | 11 | 0.44 | 6 |
| Tamil Nadu | 0.46 | 2 | 0.41 | 3 | 0.43 | 7 |
| Karnataka | 0.24 | 17 | 0.32 | 8 | 0.43 | 8 |
| Maharashtra | 0.41 | 6 | 0.35 | 6 | 0.36 | 9 |
| Orissa | 0.43 | 5 | 0.31 | 9 | 0.33 | 10 |
| Uttaranchal | 0.31 | 12 | 0.24 | 14 | 0.33 | 11 |
| Assam | 0.34 | 9 | 0.19 | 17 | 0.28 | 12 |
| Chhattisgarh | 0.14 | 20 | 0.14 | 20 | 0.28 | 13 |
| Kerala | 0.28 | 15 | 0.25 | 12 | 0.27 | 14 |
| Uttar Pradesh | 0.18 | 19 | 0.3 | 10 | 0.26 | 15 |
| Bihar | 0.26 | 16 | 0.15 | 19 | 0.24 | 16 |
| Jharkhand | 0.45 | 4 | 0.24 | 14 | 0.24 | 17 |
| Punjab | 0.3 | 13 | 0.18 | 18 | 0.24 | 18 |
| West Bengal | 0.2 | 18 | 0.25 | 12 | 0.20 | 19 |
| Rajasthan | 0.28 | 14 | 0.22 | 16 | 0.18 | 20 |

**Table 5.4**

*Overall Economic Freedom Ratings 2011*

| | 2005 | | 2009 | | 2011 | |
|---|---|---|---|---|---|---|
| *States* | *Overall* | *Rank* | *Overall* | *Rank* | *Overall* | *Rank* |
| **Gujarat** | **0.46** | **5** | **0.57** | **2** | **0.64** | **1** |
| Tamil Nadu | 0.57 | 1 | 0.59 | 1 | 0.56 | 2 |
| Madhya Pradesh | 0.49 | 2 | 0.42 | 6 | 0.55 | 3 |
| Haryana | 0.47 | 4 | 0.47 | 4 | 0.55 | 4 |
| Himachal Pradesh | 0.48 | 3 | 0.43 | 5 | 0.53 | 5 |
| Andhra Pradesh | 0.4 | 7 | 0.51 | 3 | 0.51 | 6 |
| Jammu & Kashmir | 0.34 | 15 | 0.38 | 8 | 0.47 | 7 |
| Rajasthan | 0.37 | 12 | 0.4 | 7 | 0.41 | 8 |
| Karnataka | 0.36 | 13 | 0.34 | 13 | 0.43 | 9 |
| Kerala | 0.38 | 10 | 0.36 | 10 | 0.42 | 10 |
| Chhattisgarh | 0.33 | 16 | 0.33 | 15 | 0.41 | 11 |
| Punjab | 0.41 | 6 | 0.35 | 12 | 0.40 | 12 |
| Maharashtra | 0.4 | 9 | 0.36 | 10 | 0.40 | 13 |
| Uttaranchal | 0.33 | 17 | 0.26 | 19 | 0.36 | 14 |
| Assam | 0.3 | 19 | 0.29 | 18 | 0.36 | 15 |
| Uttar Pradesh | 0.35 | 14 | 0.34 | 13 | 0.35 | 16 |
| Orissa | 0.37 | 11 | 0.31 | 17 | 0.34 | 17 |
| West Bengal | 0.31 | 18 | 0.33 | 15 | 0.32 | 18 |
| Jharkhand | 0.4 | 8 | 0.38 | 8 | 0.31 | 19 |
| Bihar | 0.25 | 20 | 0.23 | 20 | 0.29 | 20 |

We will end this chapter with quotes from Swami Vivekananda. In Swami Vivekananda's writings, there is explicit recognition of the householder as a creation of value and wealth. The means whereby that wealth is generated, and its subsequent use, is a different matter. "The householder is the basis, the prop, of the whole society. He is the principal earner. The poor, the weak, the children and the women who do not work—all live upon the householder; so there must be certain duties that he has to perform, and these duties must make him feel strong to perform them, and not make him think that he is doing things beneath his ideal. ...At the same time, he must struggle hard to acquire these things—firstly, knowledge, and secondly, wealth. It is his duty, and if he does not do his duty, he is nobody. A householder who does not struggle to get wealth is immoral. If he is lazy and content to lead an idle life, he is immoral, because upon him depend hundreds. If he gets riches, hundreds of others will be thereby supported. If there were not in this city hundreds who had striven to become rich, and who had acquired wealth, where would all this civilization, and these alms-houses and great houses be? Going after wealth in such a case is not bad, because that wealth is for distribution. The householder is the centre of life and society. It is a worship for him to acquire and spend wealth nobly, for the householder who struggles to become rich by good means and for good purposes is doing practically the same thing for the attainment of salvation as the anchorite does in his cell when he is praying."[8] Understandably, in the context of this quote, there is no difference between a household and a corporate enterprise.

"We talk foolishly against material civilization. ...Material civilization, nay, even luxury, is necessary to create work for the poor. Bread! Bread! I do not believe in a God, who cannot give me bread here, giving me eternal bliss in heaven! Pooh! India is to be raised, the poor are to be fed, education is to be spread, and the evil of priestcraft is to be removed. ..More bread, more opportunity for everybody!"[9] In different language, this is about *sattva* and *rajas* rising over *tamas* qualities. "What can bring greater strength than Sattva Guna (absolute purity of mind)? ...But I ask: How many are there in the world fortunate enough to gain that Sattva Guna? How many in this land of Bharata? ...Those amongst us who are not yet fit, but who hope to be fit, to reach to that absolutely pure Paramahamsa state—for them the acquirement of Rajas or intense activity is what is most beneficial now. Unless a man passes through Rajas, can he ever attain to that perfect Sâttvika state?"[10] Why is this relevant? Because the physical infrastructure discussion, and the social infrastructure discussion that will follow, effectively mean that Gujarat has created an enabling environment for the householder and the corporate enterprise to create wealth and transit from *tamas* qualities to the *rajas*. Having talked about physical infrastructure, in the next chapter, we move on to social infrastructure.

8. *http://www.ramakrishnavivekananda.info/vivekananda/volume_1/vol_1_frame.htm*

9. *http://www.ramakrishnavivekananda.info/vivekananda/volume_4/writings_prose/to_my_brave_boys.htm*

10. *http://www.ramakrishnavivekananda.info/vivekananda/volume_4/vol_4_frame.htm*

# 6

# Education

SINCE WE ENDED THE LAST CHAPTER with quotes from Swami Vivekananda, let us begin this chapter with Swami Vivekananda too. The flip side of wealth creation is distribution, what today goes by the name of inclusive growth. The expression 'inclusive growth' is never precisely defined and is capable of alternative interpretations. At one level, inclusive growth is about equity and ensuring that every individual in society attains a certain basic standard of living, for example, the idea that everyone should be above a certain poverty line, however defined. Once the poverty line has been defined, poverty is an absolute concept. It has nothing to do with inequality, which is a relative concept. But with inequality as a relative concept, it is capable of two completely different interpretations, with different policy implications. On the input side, one can argue that everyone should have equitable access to inputs like health, education, physical infrastructure, law and order, financial products, marketing networks, information and technology. On the output or outcome side, one can argue that everyone should have the same income. The difference between the two is a bit like saying that every student should have equal access to an educational institute (input equity) and saying that every student should obtain the same marks (output equity). In policy discussions, the difference between the two is often not made. But Swami Vivekananda was quite clear on inequality, interpreted as equality of output. "The next idea we take up is the idea of equality. These millennium ideas have been great motive powers to work. Many religions preach this as an element in them—that God is coming to rule the universe, and that then there will be no difference at all in conditions. The people who preach this doctrine are mere fanatics, and fanatics are indeed the sincerest of mankind. ...In modern times this millennial aspiration takes the form of equality—of liberty, equality, and fraternity. This is also fanaticism. True equality has never been and never can be on earth. How can we all be equal here? ....Just as inequality is necessary for creation itself, so the struggle to limit it is also necessary."[1] This is refreshingly different from the present confused discourse.

On the input side, what comes across quite clearly is the emphasis on access to education. "Education, education, education alone! Travelling through many cities of Europe and observing in them the comforts and education of even the poor people, there was brought to my mind the state of our own poor people, and I used to shed tears. What made the difference? Education was the answer I got. ...There are thousands of unselfish, kind-hearted men in our country who has renounced every thing. In the same way as they travel about and give religious instructions without any remuneration, so at least half of them can be trained as teachers or bearers of such education as we need most. For that, we want first of all a centre in the capital of each

1. *http://www.ramakrishnavivekananda.info/vivekananda/volume_1/vol_1_frame.htm*

Presidency, from whence to spread slowly throughout the whole of India."[2] But it is more than about education alone. There are novel thoughts on delivery of education and the role of ideas, even innovation. "The great difficulty in the way of educating the poor is this. Supposing even your Highness opens a free school in every village, still it would do no good, for the poverty in India is such, that the poor boys would rather go to help their fathers in the fields, or otherwise try to make a living, than come to the school. Now if the mountain does not come to Mohammed, Mohammed must go to the mountain. If the poor boy cannot come to education, education must go to him. There are thousands of single-minded, self-sacrificing Sannyâsins in our own country, going from village to village, teaching religion. If some of them can be organized as teachers of secular things also, they will go from place to place, from door to door, not only preaching, but teaching also. Suppose two of these men go to a village in the evening with a camera, a globe, some maps, etc. They can teach a great deal of astronomy and geography to the ignorant. By telling stories about different nations, they can give the poor a hundred times more information through the ear than they can get in a lifetime through books."[3]

The efficiency of different factor inputs cannot be neatly disentangled, since the efficiency of one factor input impacts on another. In addition, the efficiency of a factor input is contingent on improvements in access to physical and social infrastructure. Having said this, education is clearly important in tapping the so-called demographic dividend. There is nothing automatic about a demographic dividend materialising. Among other things, that is a function of health and education outcomes. More specifically, there is question of skills. The overall skills deficit has often been flagged. For instance, in 2002, the S.P. Gupta Special Group[4] constituted by the Planning Commission stated, "It should be noted, however, that on the average the skilled labour force at present is hardly around 6-8 per cent of the total, compared to more than 60 per cent in most of the developed and emerging developing countries." In 2001, the Montek Singh Ahluwalia Task Force,[5] again constituted by the Planning Commission, stated, "Only 5% of the Indian labour force in this age category[6] has vocational skills." While the numbers are marginally different, the Eleventh Five Year Plan document adds

2. *http://www.ramakrishnavivekananda.info/vivekananda/volume_4/vol_4_frame.htm*

3. *http://www.ramakrishnavivekananda.info/vivekananda/volume_4/vol_4_frame.htm*

4. Planning Commission (2002). *Report of the Special Group on Targeting Ten Million Employment Opportunities per year over the Tenth Plan Period*. May. http://planningcommission.nic.in/aboutus/committee/tsk_sg10m.pdf

5. Planning Commission (2001). *Report of the Task Force on Employment Opportunities*. July. *http://planningcommission.nic.in/aboutus/taskforce/tk_empopp.pdf*

6. 20-24 age-group.

the following.[7] "The NSS 61st Round results show that among persons of age 15-29 years, only about 2% are reported to have received formal vocational training and another 8% reported to have received non-formal vocational training indicating that very few young persons actually enter the world of work with any kind of formal vocational training." Among the youth, most of those with formal training are in Kerala, Maharashtra, Tamil Nadu, Himachal Pradesh and Gujarat.[8] A better indicator of a state's performance is the share of the young population that has some variety of formal training. In this, Maharashtra, Kerala, Tamil Nadu, Gujarat and Andhra Pradesh perform well. Is this because there is better training capacity and infrastructure? Is it because industrial activity exists in these states? Is it because there is a positive correlation between some minimum level of educational attainment and acquisition of formal training? The answer is probably a combination of various factors.

The Approach Paper to the Eleventh Five Year Plan[9] divides the discussion on education into five segments—elementary education, secondary education, technical/vocational education and skill development, higher/technical education and adult literacy. Adult literacy is slightly different. But the other four do not represent neat water-tight compartments, in the sense that education is a continuum and one category spills over into another. The Ministry of Human Resources Development has some data on school education. These are provisional and they are also a bit dated, since they pertain to 2009.[10] Table 6.1 is based on this and shows how Gujarat compares, benchmarked against all-India figures. Since this is meant to be illustrative, Table 6.1 has deliberately not been made exhaustive. However, Table 6.1 does tell us Gujarat has a problem with number of female teachers, the overall number of teachers and GER (gross enrolment ratios) for girls, SCs and STs. Although it does not come across that clearly in Table 6.1, there are also problems with retention and high drop-out rates and physical infrastructure. Some of Gujarat's figures may not look that bad if comparisons are made with all-India averages. However, for an economically developed state like Gujarat, is an all-India average the right benchmark to use? Or, in the area of education, should Gujarat be benchmarked against better states? Having said this, there are two additional points to be borne in mind. First, have there been temporal improvements over time and have remedial measures been taken? Table 6.2, based on the DISE dataset, clearly shows these

7. *Eleventh Five Year Plan, 2007-2012, Vol. I.*

8. NCEUS (2008). *Skill Formation and Employment Assurance in the Unorganized Sector*. August.

9. Planning Commission (2006). *Towards Faster and More Inclusive Growth, An Approach to the 11th Five Year Plan*. Government of India. December. *http://planningcommission.nic.in/plans/planrel/app11_16jan.pdf*

10. *http://mhrd.gov.in/sites/upload_files/mhrd/files/SES-School-2009-10-P.pdf*

**Table 6.1**

*Gujarat's School Education Indicators*

| *Indicator* | *Gujarat* | *All-India* |
|---|---|---|
| % of pre-primary/primary/junior basic school teachers who are trained | 100 | 86 |
| No. of female teachers/100 male teachers, pre-primary/primary/junior basic school | 64 | 86 |
| No. of female teachers/100 male teachers, higher secondary schools, inter colleges | 48 | 65 |
| Pupil/teacher ratio, pre-primary/primary/junior basic school | 30 | 42 |
| Pupil/teacher ratio, higher secondary schools, inter colleges | 41 | 39 |
| GER (Classes I-V) | 119.95 | 115.55 |
| GER for girls (Classes I-XII) | 87.29 | 84.39 |
| GER for SCs (Classes XI-XII) | 39.75 | 35.60 |
| GER for STs (Classes IX-X) | 53.72 | 49.41 |

temporal improvements.[11] Within a space of three years, improvements in some indicators are very sharp and the composite educational development index jumped from 0.584 in 2009-10 to 0.720 in 2010-11.

**Table 6.2**

*Improvement in School Indicators*

| | 2008-09 | 2010-11 |
|---|---|---|
| % single teacher schools | 2.7 | 0.86 |
| % of schools with drinking water facilities | 90.24 | 97.89 |
| % of schools with common toilets | 73.10 | 32.79 |
| % of schools with computers | 37.69 | 45.37 |
| Average number of teachers per school | 6.1 | 6.4 |
| Gross enrolment ratio, primary | 107.73 | 110.20 |
| Gross completion rate, primary | 91.60 | 96.94 |

Second, Gujarat is not a homogenous state and there is an inter-regional aspect to educational deprivation. Table 6.3 illustrates what one means.[12] As with Table 6.1, the intention is illustrative, not exhaustive. While Table 6.3 brings out the inter-district variations, because it is a snapshot, it does not bring out the sharp inter-temporal improvements. For example, in secondary education, the drop-out rate for the general category was 28.11 per cent in 2000-01 and declined to 23.77 per cent in 2011-12. For SCs, the decline was from 33.42 per cent to 25.06 per cent. And for STs, the decline was from 31.25 per cent to 26.63 per cent. On temporal improvements, here is a quote from Pratham's ASER report for rural India.[13] "Gujarat should be mentioned as a state that has also started showing a steady although slow improvement in reading levels over the last three years. One major initiative in the state for the last three years is that government officers visit randomly chosen schools to assess performance of children around November and cross check teachers' evaluations...In ASER 2011, an average of about 87% of all appointed teachers was observed to be in school on the day of the visit. Gujarat stands out with 95.6% teachers attending in primary schools." There was also a sharp decline in the number of out-of-school children between 2006 and 2011.

11. National University of Educational Planning and Administration (2012). *Elementary Education in India, Progress towards, UEE, DISE 2010-11.*

12. Directorate of Economics and Statistics (2011). *Statistical Abstract of Gujarat State 2011.* Gandhinagar: Government of Gujarat.

13. Pratham (2011). *Annual Status of Education Report (Rural), 2011.* January, *http://pratham.org/images/Aser-2011-report.pdf.* ASER also has qualitative tests of learning, which we are glossing over somewhat.

**Table 6.3**

*Drop-out Rates in Secondary Education (Classes VIII-X), 2010-11*

| District | Boys | Girls | SC Boys | SC Girls | ST Boys | ST Girls |
|---|---|---|---|---|---|---|
| Kachchh | 32.48 | 24.37 | 32.18 | 24.94 | 35.67 | 19.67 |
| Banaskantha | 57.39 | 54.47 | 63.40 | 52.62 | 54.64 | 26.63 |
| Patan | 50.01 | 28.99 | 19.57 | - 8.14 | 35.77 | - 16.67 |
| Mahesana | 33.17 | 19.96 | 40.06 | 12.61 | 71.60 | 78.40 |
| Sabarkantha | 7.05 | 8.71 | - 7.32 | 4.22 | 7.66 | 6.45 |
| Gandhinagar | 25.11 | 13.51 | 44.63 | 67.03 | 45.45 | 63.75 |
| Ahmedabad | - 4.62 | - 36.49 | 4.56 | 12.09 | 29.68 | 18.46 |
| Surendranagar | 28.45 | 33.54 | 25.74 | 30.28 | 19.64 | - 45.71 |
| Rajkot | 24.71 | 18.26 | 31.68 | 20.89 | 80.20 | 74.75 |
| Jamnagar | 43.93 | 52.37 | 55.62 | 65.26 | 63.54 | 44.90 |
| Porbandar | 5.10 | 29.95 | 13.45 | 48.44 | - 209.68 | - 100.00 |
| Junagadh | - 4.67 | 0.92 | - 76.28 | - 67.28 | - 15.64 | 6.10 |
| Amreli | - 6.33 | 29.09 | 17.76 | 49.31 | 40.32 | 50.07 |
| Bhavnagar | 71.60 | 64.59 | 82.97 | 64.22 | 78.03 | 47.45 |
| Anand | 47.30 | 38.15 | 24.63 | 53.39 | 4.32 | 38.36 |
| Kheda | 24.06 | 36.46 | 17.16 | - 10.90 | - 41.09 | - 83.93 |
| Panchmahals | 15.68 | 29.04 | 10.93 | 74.22 | 20.60 | 19.97 |
| Dohad | 21.02 | 19.53 | 26.14 | 17.97 | 18.12 | 14.81 |
| Vadodara | 18.36 | 14.68 | 19.90 | - 3.09 | 46.38 | 32.33 |
| Narmada | 28.83 | 23.99 | 16.00 | 43.75 | 31.54 | 25.54 |
| Bharuch | 23.17 | 23.88 | 19.68 | 17.54 | 44.06 | 41.95 |
| Surat | 36.68 | 34.31 | 44.78 | 51.30 | 53.07 | 51.30 |
| Dangs | 28.35 | 20.38 | 27.27 | 16.67 | 29.60 | 19.82 |
| Navsari | 6.76 | 16.40 | 57.43 | 53.55 | 41.16 | 38.11 |
| Valsad | 25.40 | 19.12 | 25.11 | 24.99 | 30.06 | 22.23 |

Consequently, if one has an impression that Gujarat does not do that well on school education, one should check the time line. Many interventions are of recent vintage and dated data do not show the improvements. One such intervention is 'Praveshotsava' and 'Rathyatra', targetted at festivals of admission, particularly for girls. Table 6.4 is symptomatic.[14] The construction of classrooms has picked up, after having flagged in the second half of the 1990s. Under the total sanitation programme and a school sanitation programme, toilets have been constructed in upper primary schools, with a

14. *http://gujarat-education.gov.in/education/about_department/achievements-1.htm*

**Table 6.4**

*Drop-out Rates*

| Year | Classes I to V | | | Classes I to VII | | |
|---|---|---|---|---|---|---|
| | *Boys* | *Girls* | *All* | *Boys* | *Girls* | *All* |
| 2003-04 | 17.79 | 17.84 | 17.83 | 36.59 | 31.44 | 33.73 |
| 2004-05 | 8.72 | 11.77 | 10.16 | 15.33 | 22.80 | 18.79 |
| 2005-06 | 4.53 | 5.79 | 5.13 | 9.97 | 14.02 | 11.82 |
| 2006-07 | 2.84 | 3.68 | 3.24 | 9.13 | 11.64 | 10.29 |
| 2007-08 | 2.77 | 3.25 | 2.98 | 8.81 | 11.08 | 9.87 |
| 2008-09 | 2.28 | 2.31 | 2.29 | 8.58 | 9.17 | 8.87 |
| 2009-10 | 2.18 | 2.23 | 2.20 | 8.33 | 8.97 | 8.65 |
| 2010-11 | 2.08 | 2.11 | 2.09 | 7.87 | 8.12 | 7.95 |
| 2011-12 | 2.05 | 2.08 | 2.07 | 7.35 | 7.82 | 7.56 |

focus on girls. Several *vidyasahayakas* have been recruited, the scheme having been introduced in 1998. The numbers are shown in Table 6.5.[15] While concerns can be expressed about para-teachers, especially if they are not trained, as an incremental improvement, para-teachers have been successfully experimented with in many states too. However, in Gujarat, *vidyasahayakas* are not para-teachers. They are properly trained, the difference with regular teachers being that they are on fixed stipend probationary contracts for five years. In 2002-03, a Vidya Laxmi Bond Scheme was started, for girls, initially in rural areas, but also extended to urban BPL (below poverty line) families. A sum of money is deposited at the time of admission (in Class I) and this is repaid with interest when the girl passes out of Class VII. Apart from this, there have been improvements in physical infrastructure, some of this under the Van Bandhu Scheme for tribal *talukas* and the Sagarkhedu Scheme for coastal *talukas*, planning facilitated by the BISAG (Bhaskaracharya Institute for space Applications and Geo-Informations) mapping mentioned earlier. Biometric monitoring of attendance has also been introduced. While more examples are unnecessary, because this is not a book on education, or school education, alone, one should mention the Gunotsav programme, designed to improve quality in 34,000 primary government schools.

The Gunotsav programme was started in 2009-10. So at one level, it is a bit too early to judge its success, at least in quantitative terms. Its novelty lies elsewhere. Ministers, including the chief minister, and senior civil servants spend an entire day at the school, evaluating its physical and educational facilities. The students are also tested and the school is graded according

15. Ibid.

**Table 6.5**

*Vidyasahayaks Appointed*

| | |
|---|---|
| 1998-99 | 15,404 |
| 1999-2000 | 20,756 |
| 2000-01 | 13,181 |
| 2001-02 | 6,900 |
| 2002-03 | 6,591 |
| 2003-04 | 3,848 |
| 2004-05 | 15,468 |
| 2005-06 | 0 |
| 2006-07 | 12,691 |
| 2007-08 | 0 |
| 2008-09 | 10,225 |
| 2009-10 | 6,294 |
| 2010-11 | 10,000 |
| 2011-12 | 11,625 |

to the qualities (*guna*). The grades are from A to F and the grading is done externally, as well as through a self-assessment by teachers. That is, there are two parallel grading exercises. Take Junagadh district as an example. Data are available for 2009-10 and 2010-11. In the external grading, in 2009-10, 0 per cent of schools in Junagadh were 'A', 2.4 per cent were 'B', 8.3 per cent were 'C', 70 per cent were 'D', 20 per cent were 'E' and 1.4 per cent were 'F'.[16] In 2010-11, these ratios changed to 0 per cent for 'A', 0.15 per cent for 'B', 19.3 per cent for 'C', 71.9 per cent for 'D', 7.5 per cent for 'E' and 1.2 per cent for 'F'. The ratings by teachers followed a similar pattern. With just two years, it is difficult to detect robust statistical trends. Nevertheless, there is a suggestion that while the movement towards 'A' or 'B' is not that marked, there has been a slight nudging upwards from 'D', 'E' and 'F' towards 'C'. The utility of the exercise is however different. It decentralises educational planning by taking administrators down to the grassroots and it also subjects schools to external scrutiny, providing feedback loops in either direction. In sum, on school education, in the last few years, there has been an additional focus and this has also been reflected in improvements in outcome indicators.

Let us now move on to the somewhat different issue of skills, often equated with vocational or technical education, though there is a low end (ITI) and a high end (IIT) to this type of education. The skills deficit in India has been flagged several times. The following drive home the point.[17] Eighty

16. Figures from Junagadh district sources.

17. Planning Commission (2008). *Eleventh Five Year Plan, 2007-2012—Vol. I: Inclusive Growth*. Government of India and Oxford University Press. These numbers are based on the 61st round (2004-05) of the NSS.

(80) per cent of new entrants into the work force have no opportunities for development of skills. While there are 12.8 million new entrants into the work force every year, the existing training capacity is 3.1 million per year. In both rural and urban India, and for both males and females, attendance rates in educational institutions drop by around 50 per cent in the age group of 15-19 years.[18] Simultaneously, labour force participation rates begin to increase in the age group of 15-19 years and by the time it comes to the age group of 25-29 years, it is 95.0 per cent for rural males and 94.4 per cent for urban males. The figures for females are lower at 36.5 per cent in rural India and 22.1 per cent in urban India. The 15-29 age group can be used as an illustration. Since post-educational institution training opportunities are limited, 87.8 per cent of the population in this bracket has had no vocational training.[19] Of the 11.3 per cent who received vocational training, only 1.3 per cent received formal vocational training.[20] Most of the skills deficit is a problem that plagues the unorganised/informal sector. While there are alternative definitions of unorganised or informal, it is unnecessary to go into those definitional problems here.[21] But it is necessary to remember that there can be workers apparently employed in the organised/formal sector, who are on informal contracts. They too are therefore unorganised/informal. In general, the organised sector has higher levels of skills than the unorganised sector and regular workers perform better than casual workers. It is worth making the point that education is not the same as skills formation, with the latter developed through some form of vocational education. Education does not necessarily lead to the development of marketable skills. However, education does provide a general template and makes it easier to access both formal and informal vocational education.

In 2004-05, NSSO (National Sample Survey Organisation) asked a question about the skill profile of the youth, defined as those between 15 and 29 years. Skills were defined as informal (both hereditary and others) and formal, formal vocational training interpreted as one where there was a structured training programme leading to a recognised certificate, diploma or degree. Understandably, formal training was higher in urban than in rural areas. However, informal skill acquisition was evenly spread across urban and rural areas. For youth, the 2004-05 survey brings out interstate differences starkly. This is shown in Table 6.6. Amongst the youth, most of those with formal training are in Uttar Pradesh, West Bengal, Gujarat, Maharashtra, Kerala,

18. The drop is sharper for rural females and is higher in rural than in urban India.

19. 85.5% for males and 90.2% for females. Understandably, the numbers without training are higher in rural areas.

20. The number is higher for males and higher in urban than in rural areas.

21. See, National Commission for Enterprises in the Unorganized Sector (NCEUS) (2007). *Report on Conditions of Work and Promotion of Livelihoods in the Unorganized Sector*. August.

Andhra Pradesh, Kerala and Tamil Nadu. A better indicator of the State's performance is the share of the young population that has some variety of formal training. In this, Himachal Pradesh, Gujarat, Maharashtra, Tamil Nadu and Kerala perform relatively better, excluding the UTs (Union Territories). Is this because there is better training capacity and infrastructure? Is it because industrial activity exists in these states? Is it because there is a positive correlation between some minimum level of educational attainment and acquisition of formal training? The answer is probably a combination of various factors. However, the dated nature of the data apart, clearly Gujarat needs to do better.

Where will these skills be needed? At an all-India level, there is some tentative identification of where these skill needs are going to be. For instance, within the services category, Planning Commission[22] identifies the following for high growth and employment—IT-enabled services, telecom services, tourism, transport services, health care, education and training, real estate and ownership of dwellings, banking and financial services, insurance, retail services and media and entertainment services. Other sectors mentioned are energy production, distribution and consumption, floriculture, construction of buildings and construction of infrastructure projects. Within industry groups are automotives, food, chemicals, basic metals, non-metallic minerals, plastic and plastic processing, leather, rubber, wood and bamboo, gems and jewellery and handicrafts, handlooms and khadi and village industries. In a separate identification from the point of view of demand for skills, there is mention of 20 sectors—automobiles and auto-components, banking/insurance and financial services, building and construction, chemicals and pharmaceuticals, construction materials/building hardware, educational and skill development services, electronics hardware, food processing/cold chain/refrigeration, furniture and furnishings, gems and jewellery, health care services, ITES or BPO, ITS or software services, leather and leather goods, media, entertainment, broadcasting, content creation and animation, organised retail, real estate services, textiles and garments, tourism, hospitality and travel trade and transportation, logistics, warehousing and packaging. Quality issues apart, these are not necessarily the skills being imparted today. And this also has a bearing on the modes through which skill development will take place. Certain elements are obvious enough. For example, one should introduce vocational education in schools, especially beyond Classes VIII. ITIs should be upgraded and extended to areas where they are absent. There should be some kind of skill development centre (SDC), if not in every block, at least in every district. However, to ensure placement, these should be done with

22. Ibid.

**Table 6.6**

*Inter-State Variations in Skill Formation Among Youth, 15-24*

| *State* | *Share of State in those with Formal Training (%)* | *% Youth in State with Formal Training* |
|---|---|---|
| Jammu & Kashmir | 0.4 | 2.0 |
| Himachal Pradesh | 1.0 | 5.6 |
| Punjab | 2.8 | 4.1 |
| Uttarakhand | 0.8 | 3.9 |
| Haryana | 2.8 | 4.5 |
| Delhi | 1.7 | 4.1 |
| Rajasthan | 2.5 | 1.7 |
| Uttar Pradesh | 6.9 | 1.7 |
| Bihar | 0.8 | 0.5 |
| Assam | 0.8 | 1.4 |
| West Bengal | 6.9 | 3.2 |
| Jharkhand | 0.8 | 1.3 |
| Orissa | 1.9 | 1.9 |
| Chhattisgarh | 2.0 | 3.5 |
| Madhya Pradesh | 3.4 | 2.2 |
| **Gujarat** | **6.6** | **4.7** |
| Maharashtra | 21.7 | 8.3 |
| Andhra Pradesh | 6.6 | 3.2 |
| Karnataka | 4.6 | 3.1 |
| Kerala | 12.2 | 15.5 |
| Tamil Nadu | 11.3 | 7.6 |
| North-East | 0.4 | 1.3 |
| Union Territories | 1.3 | 12.6 |

the involvement of the private sector, such as in the PPP (public private partnership) mode, and not by the government alone.

However, it must also be recognised that there are several layers in the skills problem. Nor are there clear answers as to the superiority, or otherwise, of public delivery *vis-à-vis* private delivery.[23] There are PPP models in several countries in Europe. In Japan, training is essentially provided through the enterprise, whereas in East Asia, delivery is fundamentally public. At the

23. See the discussion in, Asian Development Bank (2004). *Improving Technical Education and Vocational Training, Strategies for Asia.*

other end, in Britain and USA, delivery is primarily private. Vocational education through schools works well in USA, Sweden, France, South Korea and Taiwan. Formal employment is low in India and several parallel systems co-exist—the formal public (government) training system, public training that caters to the informal sector, the non-government (both private and NGO (non-governmental organisations)) network of formal training institutions and the non-government (primarily NGO-driven) system of informal training. In the first category one has vocational education through schools,[24] polytechnics through the Ministry of Human Resource Development, the Craftsmen Training Scheme and the Apprenticeship Training Scheme through the Directorate General for Employment and Training under the Ministry of Labour and Employment. The plans to expand public capacity under the 'National Skill Development Policy' are essentially under this segment. In the second segment of public training that caters to the informal sector, one has community polytechnics run by the Ministry of Human Resource Development, the JSS (Jan Shikshan Sansthan) for disadvantaged adults,[25] the NIOS (National Institute of Open Schooling), Ministry of Labour and Employment's Skill Development Initiative,[26] Ministry of Micro, Small and Medium Enterprises' entrepreneurship development programmes and entrepreneurship skill development programmes, PMRY (Prime Minister's Rozgar Yojana),[27] the SJSRY (Swarna Jayanti Shahari Rojgar Yojana),[28] the SGSY (Swarnajayanti Gram Swarozgar Yojana)[29] and Department of Rural Development's RUDSETIs (Rural Development and Self-Employment Training Institutes).[30] Ministry of Textiles, Development Commissioner (Handicrafts), Ministry of Youth Affairs and Sports, Ministry of Women and Child Development, Department of Science and Technology, Ministry of Agriculture, Ministry of Health and Family Welfare, Ministry of Tourism, Ministry of Food Processing, Ministry of Social Justice and Empowerment and Ministry of Minority Affairs also have small programmes with some skill development components. There can be skills deficits that are structural in nature. These require candidates to go through longer duration training. In other instances, shorter duration interventions will work. And in the last category, all that is required is last mile unemployability.

24. Especially +2 in secondary schools. A centrally sponsored scheme has existed since 1988. Such training is followed by apprentice training under the Apprenticeship Act.

25. This can be implemented by NGOs.

26. This was started in 2007.

27. This was started in 1993 and has an element of training for self-employed entrepreneurs.

28. This was started in 1997 and has an element of training in urban areas. It has two separate components for self-employment and wage employment.

29. This also has a training component.

30. The first RUDSETI was set up in Karnataka in 1982. Ministry of Rural Development also has pilots in partnership with IL&FS.

Against this background, unlike school education, there is no demonstrated market failure for technical or higher education, though one can empathise with the state government's intent to increase capacity in ITIs and polytechnics and also towards the higher end of the technical training ladder (engineering, pharmacy). This is also understandable, since some of this upgradation is linked to external funding (Union government, World Bank). Interpreted thus, the experiment of switching 72 of the 253 ITIs to a PPP mode is more interesting. Perhaps, the only exception to that general statement about market failure is for state intervention for specific backward segments, such as the KVKs (Kaushalya Vardhan Kendras) (launched in 2010-2011) targetted at women or special vocational training programmes targetted at tribal youth. But in all fairness, it is not that the principle of private sector involvement is not recognised. For example, some VTCs (vocational training centres) for tribal youth are in the PPP mode. But it is also fair to say that this has not picked up that much steam yet.

Having said this, there are a few initiatives one should flag. First, the Gujarat Knowledge Society, in PPP mode, offers short-duration training. Second, there is the SCOPE (Society for Creation of Opportunity through Proficiency in English). Third, there are mini ITIs and polytechnics. Fourth, the open school system apart, Gujarat is the only state which has integrated ITI education with mainstream education. That is, depending on exit (Standard VIII or X), one takes a language exam, and after having completed ITI training, is eligible for college admissions.

We should also mention the question of matching labour supply to labour demand, something that employment exchanges were supposed to do. Unorganised sector male wage employment is primarily in manufacturing, construction, trading and transport. For women, trading and transport can be replaced by domestic services. How do these workers find out jobs are available and decide on temporary or permanent migration? The answer is simple. Barring limited instances of job offers at factory gates, there are only two channels: informal (family, caste, community) networks and labour contractors. This kind of information dissemination cannot be efficient, apart from commissions, exploitative or otherwise, paid to agents. Other than such disintermediation and information dissemination being inefficient, there can be no question of skill formation if recruitment is through such informal channels. Clearly, one needs efficient clearing houses that match supply and demand. Employment exchanges have failed to do this successfully in most states, Gujarat being an exception. They have succeeded in a very limited way with jobs for the private sector and increasingly less with jobs for the public sector. For the private sector, the mandatory requirement of recruitment through employment exchanges only applies below a threshold level of wages and these have not been revised for years. Whatever the law may say *de jure*, there is nothing mandatory about employment exchanges *de facto*. For the public sector, a Supreme Court judgement in 1996 said that appointments no longer had to be from the pool that was registered with employment exchanges, as long as job vacancies were suitably publicised. The public sector also set up channels like Staff Selection Commissions, Banking Service Commissions and Railway Recruitment Boards. Administration and expenditure on employment exchanges are now state subjects, an earlier matching grant from the centre having run its course in 1969. So there should be a cost-benefit analysis of the employment exchanges. Do placements justify the expenditure on them? Gujarat is an example of a state that has tried to reform the 41 employment exchanges, with some PPP kind of involvement.[31] Job fairs have also been held to perform the matching function. Under UDISHA, there are placement cells in colleges.

While there is no denying these positives, including the idea of the knowledge consortium of Gujarat for higher education, for technical and higher education, one can not avoid the sense that there is greater scope for the government to step back. Including agricultural universities, there are 21 state universities in Gujarat, 3 Central universities, 16 private universities and 6 institutes of national importance. However, the private ones still tend to be specialised, with a professional focus. Is there scope for these to expand and for the state to withdraw? The large number of private universities set up in the last 10 years suggests that the answer is in the affirmative. Such changes can be supply-driven, or react to demand. The increases in enrolment in school education imply that the demand for change will come, perhaps 10 years down the line, and drive a clear focus in government delivery, away from technical and higher education, towards school education. Subsidising the poor and the disadvantaged through government financing is a different proposition altogether.

31. These are called Rozgar Sahay Kendras in Gujarat, labelled as PPP. The public employment exchange provides a database of people on the register (the supply of labour, so to speak) and the private agency matches it with demand.

# 7

# Health

THE CASE FOR MARKET FAILURE is generally greater for health than it is for education. If there is a perception that Gujarat does not do that well in social sectors, that is truer of health than of education. However, before turning to Gujarat-specific issues, some general comments are in order.

In September 2010, India's Ministry of Health and Family Welfare presented an annual report on the state of India's health, presumably the first of several such status reports.[1] There is a self-congratulatory under-current in this report. Life expectancy has increased to 63.5 years. Infant and under-5 mortality rates have declined, with the IMR (infant mortality rate) at 53 per 1000 live births. Subject to data problems about MMR (maternal mortality ratio), that too has dropped to 254 per 100,000 live births. All these are 2009 figures. For Gujarat, this reports a life expectancy of 64.1 years, IMR of 50 and a MMR of 160. However, Gujarat's IMR has dropped to 44 in 2010. The respective all-India figures are 63.5 years, 53 and 254. If Gujarat's benchmark is better performing states, as it should be, and not all-India averages, obviously Gujarat needs to do better. The *Mid-Term Appraisal of the Eleventh Five Year Plan* reports that 54.0 per cent of Gujarat's children were immunised in 2002-04 and the figure went up to 54.9 per cent in 2007-2008.[2] For all-India, the respective numbers were 45.9 per cent and 54.1 per cent. To state the obvious, the numbers are dated, not just for Gujarat, but for all states. A NRHM (National Rural Health Mission) was launched in 2005 and for Gujarat, the NHRM site also mentions that the sex ratio is 920, compared to 933 for India.[3]

There are several problems with any self-congratulatory under-current. First, depending on the country with which one is making comparisons, India is still an underperformer in health. Second, there is a 2009 country report on India's progress towards the MDGs (Millennium Development Goals).[4] The MDG system has a hierarchy of goals, targets and indicators and several are on health. Stated simply, in terms of progress towards 2015, India performs far better on poverty reduction and education than it does on any of the health-related indicators. While lauding Gujarat on achieving the poverty reduction MDG targets, this MDG report also states, "The rural-urban divide in incidence of infant mortality is quite glaring," and mentions a Gujarat

1. Ministry of Health and Family Welfare (2010). *Annual Report to the People on Health*. India. September, *http://mohfw.nic.in/showfile.php?lid=121*

2. *http://planningcommission.nic.in/plans/mta/11th_mta/chapterwise/chap7_health.pdf*

3. *http://mohfw.nic.in/NRHM/State%20Files/gujarat.htm*

4. There have been two earlier reports too. But this 2009 is the latest. Central Statistical Organisation (2009). *Millennium Development Goals, India Country Report 2009: Mid-Term Statistical Appraisal*. New Delhi: Ministry of Statistics and Programme Implementation. *http://mospi.nic.in/rept%20_%20pubn/ftest.asp?rept_id=ssd04_2009&type=NSSO*

differential of 24. Third, progress has to be benchmarked against what was expected or projected. The Eleventh Five Year Plan (2007-2012) had projected that by 2012, the MMR would be 100 and the IMR would be 28. On the assumption that these were then believed to be deliverable targets, there has been slippage.

Since the Bhore Committee of 1946, there have been 21 committees and commissions with a direct focus on health, not counting the ones that deal with pharmaceuticals or related areas.[5] The recommendations of these committees and commissions helped to shape India's health care infrastructure, policy and legislation. Let us highlight two of these recommendations, because they did argue for choice, competition and efficiency on the supply-side and an end to public sector monopolies, with suggestions on financing health care. It is a different matter that these recommendations were not implemented and also that those recommendations were made in 1946 and 1948.

In 1946, there was the Health Survey and Development (Bhore) Committee, which recommended a public health service and the present PHC (Public Health Centres) and CHC (Community Health Centres) system. But the committee also stated, "The following questions seem, at the outset, to require an answer: (1) Whether the service should be free or paid for by the recipient: if the latter, whether it should be a graded scale of payment so as to suit the level of the patient's income and whether such payment should be made for each occasion when service is rendered or through some form of sickness insurance; (2) Whether our scheme should be based on a full-time salaried service of doctors or on private practitioners resident in each local area or settled there on a subsidy basis; (3) Whether, in either case, some measure of choice can be given to the patient as regards his doctor" (Vol. II, p.21). In 1948, the sub-committee on National Health (Sokhey Committee) of the National Planning Committee stated, "The availability of medical benefits or nursing service should not depend upon an individual's ability to pay for them but that they should be made available equally irrespective of that ability, as a matter of common obligation of the state towards its members. Those members themselves may indeed, quite legitimately, be required to contribute according to their ability, in one form, or another, to the improvement in their health and living conditions. But irrespective of that contribution, the state must accept the obligation to provide at least a standard minimum of organized health service, including advice and treatment to every suffering member of the community. ... But in so far as active assistance, in the shape of direct financial provision from the

5. In a collaborative exercise between the MoHFW (Ministry of Health and Family Welfare) and the WHO (World Health Organization) (India), the reports of most of these committees/commissions are available at *http://nrhm-mis.nic.in/ui/who/GOI-who-link.htm*

public purse is concerned on hospitals, dispensaries, professional advice, technical apparatus or even sanatoria, nursing homes, asylums for mentally defective, this should be as far as possible derived from the contribution of the individuals insured. It is a healthy principle not only because it teaches people to attend themselves to avoidable causes or conditions of disease; it is psychologically still more valuable because it teaches self-help, eliminates any taint of charity or unearned dole not specifically contributed to by the individual concerned is apt to engender."

The NRHM (National Rural Health Mission) has already been mentioned. While its focus was on improving the health care infrastructure in rural India, the emphasis was primarily on child birth and pre-natal care. For example, the specific targets are about IMR (this includes vaccination), MMR, TFR (total fertility rate), undernutrition among children, anaemia among women and girls (this includes the provision of nutritional supplements), provision of clean drinking water and raising the sex ratio in the 0-6 age group. That is because the RCH (reproductive and child health) programme was a key building block of NRHM.

The NCMH (National Commission on Macroeconomics and Health) had some reliable data on major health conditions in terms of their contribution to India's disease burden, though it did not disaggregate this state-wise.[6] This is shown in Table 7.1.[7] Category I health conditions accounted for almost half the disease burden in Table 7.1. Some of these pre-transition diseases are declining in importance. However, there are question marks about HIV/AIDS, some variants of TB and drug-resistant malaria. Correspondingly, Category II health conditions like cardio vascular disease, diabetes, respiratory conditions like asthma and COPD (chronic obstructive pulmonary disease) and mental health disorders are increasing in importance. Category III (accidents and injuries) have also been increasing. The problem is that a heterogeneous country like India, marked by disparities, is both in pre-transition and post-transition stages.

The core of the delivery problem is in rural India, where primary health care is provided through a network of sub-centres, PHCs and CHCs. Table 7.2 is based on Central data.[8] There are population norms for such sub-centres, PHCs and CHCs. For instance, a population size of 5,000 must have a sub-centre, a population size of 30,000 must have a PHC and a population size of

6. National Commission of Macroeconomic and Health (2005). *Disease Burden in India: Estimations and Causal Analysis. http://www.whoindia.org/LinkFiles/Commision_on_Macroeconomic_and_Health_Bg_P2_Burden_of_Disease_Estimations_and_Casual_analysis.pdf*

7. Though use was made of NSS (National Sample Survey) data from 1995-96, and NSS data from 2004-05 (but not later) are now available, there are unlikely to be major changes to Table 7.1.

8. *http://mohfw.nic.in/NRHM/State%20Files/gujarat.htm*

**Table 7.1**

*Health Conditions and DALYs (Disability-Adjusted Life-Years) Lost*

| *Disease/Health Condition* | *DALYs Lost (X 1000)* | *Share in Total Burden of Disease (%)* |
|---|---|---|
| TB | 7,577 | 2.8 |
| HIV/AIDS | 5,611 | 2.11 |
| Diarrheal diseases | 22,005 | 8.2 |
| Malaria and other vector-borne conditions | 4,200 | 1.6 |
| Leprosy | 208 | 0.1 |
| Childhood diseases | 14,463 | 5.4 |
| Otitis media | 475 | 0.1 |
| Maternal and peri-natal conditions | 31,207 | 11.6 |
| Other communicable, maternal & pre-natal diseases | 49,517 | 18.4 |
| Cancer | 8,992 | 3.4 |
| Diabetes | 1,981 | 0.7 |
| Mental illness | 22,944 | 8.5 |
| Blindness | 3,699 | 1.4 |
| Cardiovascular diseases | 26,932 | 10.0 |
| COPD and asthma | 4,061 | 1.5 |
| Oral disease | 1,247 | 0.5 |
| Other non-communicable diseases | 18,801 | 7.0 |
| Injuries | 45,032 | 16.7 |
| Unlisted conditions | 68,319 | 25.4 |

120,000 must have a CHC.[9] A sub-centre has a lady ANM (auxiliary nurse/mid-wife) and a MHW (male health worker). There is a LHV (lady health visitor) for six such sub-centres. The PHC is a referral unit for six sub-centres and has a MO (medical officer) and other staff. The CHCs are supposed to have four medical specialists (surgeon, physician, gynaecologist, paediatrician), with an anaesthetist and eye surgeon eventually made mandatory. In parallel with the NRHM, a NUHM (National Urban Health Mission) has now been proposed. The Ministry of Health's Annual Report succinctly states the problem in urban India.[10] "However, while there is somewhat a uniform public health infrastructure in the rural areas, it is largely non-existent in urban areas except in some large urban centres and metropolitan cities that too mostly

9. These have been the norms since 2009. However, there are lower population thresholds for hilly and tribal areas.

10. *op.cit.* no. 1.

**Table 7.2**

*Gujarat's Health Infrastructure*

| *Particulars* | *Required* | *In Shortfall* | *Position* |
|---|---|---|---|
| Sub-centre | 7263 | 7274 | - |
| PHC | 1172 | 1073 | 99 |
| CHC | 293 | 273 | 20 |
| Multipurpose Worker (Female)/ANM at sub-centres and PHCs | 8347 | 7060 | 1287 |
| Health Worker (Male) MPW(M) at sub-centres | 7274 | 4456 | 2818 |
| Health Assistant (Female)/LHV at PHCs | 1073 | 267 | 806 |
| Health Assistant (Male) at PHCs | 1073 | 2421 | - |
| Doctor at PHCs | 1073 | 1019 | 54 |
| Obstetricians and Gynaecologists at CHCs | 273 | 6 | 267 |
| Physicians at CHCs | 273 | 0 | 273 |
| Paediatricians at CHCs | 273 | 6 | 267 |
| Total Specialists at CHCs | 1092 | 81 | 1011 |
| Radiographers | 273 | 124 | 149 |
| Pharmacist | 1346 | 781 | 565 |
| Laboratory Technicians | 1346 | 897 | 449 |
| Nurse/Midwife | 2984 | 1585 | 1399 |

focused on reproductive and child health services. Approximately three-quarters of urban healthcare is accounted for by private health facilities and therefore, result in substantial out of pocket expenses. The health indicators for the urban poor are as bad as their rural counterparts and much worse than the urban average. Poor environmental condition in the slums along with high population density makes them vulnerable to various communicable and vector borne diseases...The poor health outcomes can partially be traced to the inadequate services, like water supply and sanitation, and housing facilities."

The focus thus is on public sector delivery, both in rural and in urban India, despite the statement that three-quarters of urban health care is accounted for by the private sector. However, some empirical work by Jishnu Das shows that even in rural India, access is primarily through the private sector. "Typically, households can access multiple providers, ranging from fully qualified public and private sector providers to those without any formal medical training in the private sector...According to a recent report, across rural India, the average household can access 3.2 private, 0.3 public, and 2.3 public paramedical staff within their village. ...Of those identified as doctors, 65% had no formal medical training and, of every 100 visits to health care providers, eight were to the public sector and 70 to untrained private sector providers."[11] For example, in rural Gujarat, on an average, 1.19 private providers are available within a village, with 0.25 public doctors and 3.49 non-doctor public providers. The report in question is an important one, because it demolishes the proposition that there is a market failure of health workers in rural India and that the public sector must fill the void.[12] Contrary to *a priori* expectations, the key trends are the following. First, the availability of medical providers in rural India is quite high, nearly 6 available per rural village. Second, more than 50 per cent of medical providers are private providers. However, third, the majority of medical providers have no medical qualifications. Sixty-five (65) per cent have no formal medical training. Fourth, most households visit private doctors and doctors with no medical qualifications.[13] Ninety-two (92) per cent go to private providers and 79 per cent go to unqualified providers.

A private market thus exists. The problem is with its quality and lack of regulation. In contrast, the public sector provisioning may not have problems of regulation, but it continues to have problems of access and quality. It is because of this lack of service quality in public sector delivery, spliced with the non-availability of drugs, that patients resort to the private sector.

In ad hoc fashion, several States have also experimented with PPP (public private partnership) models in delivering health care, outsourcing and levy of appropriate user charges. The MoHFW has a database that collated these and other reform attempts.[14] Gujarat itself has experimented with user charges. Typically, such charges are imposed for diagnostic and curative services on patients above the poverty line, while those below the poverty line are exempted and continue to receive free and subsidised services. Gujarat's government hospitals and CHCs have Rogi Kalyan Samitis, which are explicitly expected to outsource non-core activities. Simultaneously, the Gujarat Medical Service Corporation Limited was set up to procure bulk generic drugs. In the course of formulating the Eleventh Five Year Plan (2007–2012), the Planning Commission constituted a task force on PPP to improve

11. Das, Jishnu (2011). "The Quality of Medical-Care in Low Income Countries: From Providers to Markets", *PLOS (Public Library of Science) Medicine*. April.

12. The MAQARI (Medical Advice, Quality, and Availability in Rural India) Team and CPR Policy Brief (2011). *Mapping Medical Providers in Rural India: Four Key Trends*. February. *http://cprindia.org/sites/default/files/policy%20brief_1.pdf*

13. The word 'doctor' is being used in loose fashion. It does not imply the possession of a MBBS degree.

14. Ministry of Health and Family Welfare (MoHFW) (2007). *Health Sector Policy Reform Options Database of India (HS-PROD)*. New Delhi: Government of India.

health care delivery.[15] Instead of the classic obsession with increasing public expenditure and assuming that it must be equated with public provisioning, the task force's report indicates how choice and competition can be introduced. The report begins by accepting the inevitable, instead of questioning it, namely, the importance of the private sector, both for profit and non-profit. This does not negate the point about lack of regulation, since the quality of health care provided by the private sector varies. In general, private health care services are also more expensive than public ones, more so for in-patient services. Services can also be contracted out on a temporary basis to the private sector. The government can pay an outside agency to manage a specific function, or government facilities can be leased to private entities. Subsidies meant for the poor can be routed through private entities. While there can be no universal template, there are two propositions that are clearly myths—first, everything has to be delivered by the public sector; second, the poor are unwilling to pay. The usual approach to addressing health problems is one of increasing public expenditure on health, the argument being that OOP (out-of-pocket) expenditure on health care is too high. While this is true, this is more of an insurance issue and its delivery.

Since insurance has been mentioned, let us flag this first. The RSBY (Rashtriya Swasthya Bima Yojana) is a centrally sponsored health insurance scheme, meant for BPL (below poverty line) households, with a matching contribution by the state government. The BPL data have to conform to Planning Commission specifications. Started on a pilot basis in 5 districts in 2008-09, this now covers 1.9 million rural BPL families and in 2011-12, was extended to 1 million urban BPL families too. Through smart cards, this ensures cashless treatment in recognised hospitals, not just public, but private too. Since the public health care infrastructure is weak, as has been mentioned earlier, the Gujarat government's Chiranjivi Yojana also taps the private sector, to employ private sector specialists in safe delivery. While the poor household does not have to pay, the government pays the private sector specialist. The Chiranjivi Yojana was first introduced on pilot basis in 2005 and has picked up since then. For example, there were 7,793 beneficiaries in 2005-06 and 150,979 in 2010-11. The Chiranjivi Yojana has won several awards. The Bal Sakha Yojana has a similar PPP idea. It was launched in 2009 and covers all BPL households and tribal households, even if they happen to be APL (above povety line). Neo-natal care is provided by private enrolled peadiatricians, who are then reimbursed by the state. Finally, there is the recently launched Mukhyamantri Amrutam Yojana, to cover some categories of hospitalisation and surgery for BPL households, through empanelled health care providers, public or private.

15. Planning Commission (2007). *Draft Report on Recommendations of Task Force on Public Private Partnership for the 11th Plan*. Government of India. *http://planningcommission.nic.in/plans/planrel/11thf.htm*.

Health care has several dimensions. There is the preventive part, interpreted as clean drinking water, sanitation, sewage treatment and nutrition, be it through MDMS (Mid-day Meal Scheme), ICDS (Integration Child Development Scheme), vitamin supplements or otherwise. Incidentally, in ULBs, Gujarat has several pay and use toilets in BOT mode. There is a KPSY (Kasturba Poshan Sahay Yojana) for nutrition during pregnancy. There is also the preventive part, interpreted as immunisation. The state government's focus has clearly been on reducing neo-natal deaths and bringing down the IMR and MMR. That is where the JSY (Janani Suraksha Yojana) comes in, designed to shift poor women to institutional delivery. The number of JSY beneficiaries went up from 12,573 in 2005-06 to 342,211 in 2011-12.[16] Simultaneously, the percentage of institutional deliveries has sharply gone up from 55.87 per cent in 2003-04 to 93.66 per cent in 2011-12. Immunisation coverage has also increased. Obviously, this is not because of JSY alone. JSY should be considered in conjunction with the JSSK (Janani Shishu Suraksha Karyakram), a CSS for subsidised delivery and treatment for infants. There has been an IMNCI (Integrated Management of New Born and Childhood Illness), launched in 2005, combined with Mamta (Malnutrition Assessment and Monitoring to Act) initiatives, which effectively register a mother and child and track post-natal nutrition, health and immunisation status. E-Mamta computerises this tracking. The Mamta Abhiyan has for separate components—Mamta Divas (Health and Nutrition Day), Mamta Mulakat (post-natal-care visits), Mamta Sandarbh (referral services) and Mamta Nondh (recording and reporting). Perhaps the most interesting of all these experiments is the emergency 108 number, which is not just for medical emergencies, but for police and fire emergencies too. This was launched in 2007 and is operated by GVK EMRI (Emergency Management and Research Institute). There are now 506 ambulances and all districts have been covered. On an average, there are between 2000 and 2,200 (108) calls every day. Data are dated. When more current data come in, these interventions should logically show declines in both IMR and MMR. It is undeniable that Gujarat's base in health care outcomes was low. It is also true that the dated

16. *http://www.gujhealth.gov.in/janani-suraksha.htm*

data reveal this. But as more recent data come in, these interventions should show improvements.

There remains the matter of the sex ratio and the PC & PNDT (Pre-conception and Pre-Natal Diagnostics Techniques) Act and its enforcement, or lack. Table 7.3 shows the sex ratios. Gujarat's sex ratios are well below national averages, though the decline has been less sharp between 2001 and 2011. What is important is not the overall sex ratio, as in Table 7.3, but the child

**Table 7.3**

*Sex Ratios*

| | *1951* | *1961* | *1971* | *1981* | *1991* | *2001* | *2011* |
|---|---|---|---|---|---|---|---|
| **Gujarat** | **952** | **940** | **934** | **942** | **934** | **920** | **918** |
| Kachchh | 1079 | 1041 | 1012 | 999 | 964 | 942 | 907 |
| Banaskantha | 951 | 947 | 941 | 947 | 934 | 930 | 936 |
| Patan | 971 | 956 | 957 | 963 | 944 | 932 | 935 |
| Mahesana | 1003 | 974 | 961 | 974 | 951 | 927 | 925 |
| Sabarkantha | 973 | 954 | 965 | 976 | 965 | 947 | 950 |
| Gandhinagar | 992 | 961 | 936 | 943 | 935 | 913 | 920 |
| Ahmedabad | 836 | 852 | 863 | 888 | 897 | 892 | 903 |
| Surendranagar | 958 | 943 | 941 | 934 | 921 | 924 | 929 |
| Rajkot | 988 | 963 | 947 | 947 | 946 | 930 | 924 |
| Jamnagar | 986 | 952 | 942 | 949 | 949 | 941 | 938 |
| Porbandar | 1001 | 962 | 952 | 967 | 960 | 946 | 947 |
| Junagadh | 976 | 949 | 933 | 954 | 960 | 955 | 952 |
| Amreli | 974 | 959 | 957 | 980 | 985 | 987 | 964 |
| Bhavnagar | 955 | 936 | 941 | 954 | 944 | 937 | 931 |
| Anand | 906 | 890 | 880 | 905 | 912 | 910 | 921 |
| Kheda | 918 | 914 | 907 | 924 | 924 | 923 | 937 |
| PanchMahals | 922 | 925 | 930 | 942 | 934 | 938 | 945 |
| Dohad | 954 | 954 | 964 | 984 | 976 | 985 | 986 |
| Vadodara | 914 | 906 | 900 | 915 | 913 | 919 | 934 |
| Narmada | 938 | 952 | 961 | 954 | 947 | 949 | 960 |
| Bharuch | 946 | 945 | 944 | 938 | 925 | 921 | 924 |
| The Dangs | 877 | 913 | 946 | 970 | 983 | 987 | 1007 |
| Navsari | 1041 | 1030 | 1002 | 975 | 958 | 955 | 961 |
| Valsad | 1001 | 1005 | 992 | 989 | 957 | 920 | 926 |
| Surat | 973 | 967 | 943 | 908 | 882 | 810 | 788 |
| Tapi | 959 | 972 | 957 | 989 | 987 | 996 | 1004 |

**Table 7.4**

*Size of Government State Ratings and Rankings*

| States | 2005 Area1 | 2005 Rank | 2009 Area1 | 2009 Rank | 2011 Area1 | 2011 Rank |
|---|---|---|---|---|---|---|
| Haryana | 0.50 | 7 | 0.63 | 3 | 0.75 | 1 |
| **Gujarat** | **0.56** | **2** | **0.69** | **1** | **0.74** | **2** |
| Maharashtra | 0.52 | 5 | 0.53 | 6 | 0.68 | 3 |
| Assam | 0.41 | 11 | 0.51 | 7 | 0.63 | 4 |
| Jammu & Kashmir | 0.31 | 20 | 0.43 | 14 | 0.63 | 5 |
| Punjab | 0.49 | 8 | 0.54 | 5 | 0.61 | 6 |
| West Bengal | 0.52 | 4 | 0.58 | 4 | 0.61 | 7 |
| Andhra Pradesh | 0.39 | 12 | 0.49 | 8 | 0.58 | 8 |
| Tamil Nadu | 0.46 | 9 | 0.47 | 11 | 0.57 | 9 |
| Himachal Pradesh | 0.58 | 1 | 0.48 | 10 | 0.56 | 10 |
| Bihar | 0.38 | 16 | 0.44 | 12 | 0.54 | 11 |
| Kerala | 0.51 | 6 | 0.49 | 8 | 0.54 | 12 |
| Chhattisgarh | 0.37 | 17 | 0.32 | 19 | 0.53 | 13 |
| Jharkhand | 0.56 | 3 | 0.67 | 2 | 0.50 | 14 |
| Rajasthan | 0.34 | 18 | 0.44 | 12 | 0.50 | 15 |
| Karnataka | 0.38 | 15 | 0.36 | 16 | 0.48 | 16 |
| Uttaranchal | 0.39 | 13 | 0.25 | 20 | 0.45 | 17 |
| Orissa | 0.32 | 19 | 0.38 | 15 | 0.44 | 18 |
| Madhya Pradesh | 0.39 | 14 | 0.35 | 17 | 0.42 | 19 |
| Uttar Pradesh | 0.45 | 10 | 0.33 | 18 | 0.40 | 20 |

sex ratio, which is worst in districts like Surat, Gandhinagar and Mahesana. These are relatively more prosperous districts and as with elsewhere in India, there is a positive correlation between female feticide and income, infanticide being a slightly different issue. However, beyond awareness and stronger enforcement of the PC & PNDT Act, it is difficult to see what can be done. This is essentially what the Beti Vadhavo Abhiyan is about. After all, one is talking about complicated socio-economic and cultural phenomena, reflective of the status of women.

Finally, let us revisit the economic freedom rating mentioned earlier. To recapitulate, it is based on three heads, size of government, legal structure and security of property rights and regulation of labour and business, with an overall or aggregate ranking too. Earlier, we have flagged Gujarat's performance on the aggregate and the regulation of labour and business head, the latter underlining freedom granted to private initiative. Table 7.4 shows Gujarat's performance on size of government. In such rankings, there is a normative presumption that the lower the importance of government, the better it is. This value judgement is not without qualifications. For example, many social sector interventions, such as in areas of education and health, require public expenditure, often of the revenue kind. In the presence of market failures, and both education and health have examples of these, it is unrealistic to expect that the private sector will step in. Having said this, Gujarat's scores (though not the ranks between 2009 and 2011) show an improvement on size of government. In any event, in several health sector interventions, there has been a reliance on private sector initiatives. More accurately, that reliance has been on private sector provisioning, not private sector financing. The financing, especially for BPL households, has still largely been public, including through insurance. This is certain to change, once income growth takes households out of the BPL category.

# 8

# Deprivation and the ST Issue

THE PLANNING COMMISSION set up an Expert Group on development challenges in extremism affected areas and this submitted a report in 2008.[1] Right towards the beginning, this report states, "The main support for the Naxalite movement comes from dalits and adivasis," and this is undeniably the case. "While there is no simple correspondence between the areas under Naxalite influence and the proportion of Dalits and Adivasis in the population, it is the case that these areas generally have relatively high Dalit or Adivasi concentration." The report then goes on to mention the development and governance deficits and deprivation problems among SCs/STs, issues of political marginalisation, human rights violations, crimes and atrocities against SCs in rural India, lack of access to traditional resources among ST populations and inadequate grievance redressal through the judicial system. Though deprivation among SCs is indeed an issue, it is also true that the Naxalite movement is primarily a ST phenomenon. STs tend to be geographically concentrated and live in geographically contiguous areas, which is also the reason why the Fifth Schedule of the Constitution provides for the declaration of certain areas as Scheduled Areas. The Sixth Schedule tribal areas in the North-East are somewhat different in nature. For STs in the non-North-Eastern parts of India, there is collective deprivation because of an inadequate supply of public goods and services, partly explained by inaccessibility of terrain. Simultaneously, that geographical proximity also facilitates collective expression of discontent.

Here are a few quotes about Gujarat from the *India Human Development Report*.[2] "The demographic composition within the state shows that STs and SCs accounted for more than one-fourth of the state's population... The incidence of poverty among STs is higher than the state average... Looking at the other human development outcome indicators, particularly health indicators, the performance of STs in Gujarat is worse than at the national level, and also worse than other social groups within the state. This is primarily due to the fact that they are concentrated in rural areas, where the public health facilities are not as good as the facilities available in urban areas...The literacy rate among STs is the lowest among all the social groups in the state...Since STs constitute about 17 per cent of the state's population, their low literacy rate is a matter of serious concern." The intention of this chapter is not to revisit social sector issues, which we have already done, but to focus on something else. For the moment, 17 per cent of Gujarat's population consists of STs and STs are substantially worse off compared to any other social group.

1. Planning Commission (2008). *Development Challenges in Extremist Affected Areas*. April. *http://planningcommission.nic.in/reports/publications/rep_dce.pdf*. The Expert Group was set up in 2006.

2. Planning Commission (2011). *India Human Development Report 2011: Towards Social Inclusion*. New Delhi: Institute of Applied Manpower Research and Oxford University Press.

District-wise, ST figures are still not available from the 2011 Census. From the 2001 Census, we know that 14.8 per cent of Gujarat's population was ST.[3] For districts, the figures were 8.2 per cent for Kachchh, 8.2 per cent for Banaskantha, 20.2 per cent for Sabarkantha, 27.5 per cent for Panchmahals, 72.3 per cent for Dohad, 26.6 per cent for Vadodara, 78.1 per cent for Narmada, 32.4 per cent for Bharuch, 28.2 per cent for Surat, 93.8 per cent for the Dangs, 48.1 per cent for Navsari and 54.8 per cent for Valsad.[4] There is a long tradition of identifying backward districts, within the government and outside it. After all, there are considerable developmental variations within a State too, particularly if it happens to be a large and heterogeneous State. One such non-government identification of India's backward districts was done several years ago, based on indicators linked to the Millennium Development Goals.[5] Under some criteria, this identified Anand, Banaskantha, Dohad, Junagadh, Kachchh, Kheda, Navsari, Panchmahals, Porbandar, Rajkot, Sabarkantha, Surat, Surendranagar, the Dangs, Vadodara and Valsad as backward. The criteria are not important. What is important is that there is a correlation between ST populations and backwardness of a district.

The Annual Report of the Ministry of Home Affairs has a table on incidents of left-wing extremist violence between 2008 and 2011.[6] The states that figure in this list are Andhra Pradesh, Bihar, Chhattisgarh, Jharkhand, Madhya Pradesh, Maharashtra, Odisha, Uttar Pradesh and West Bengal. There is also an Integrated Action Plan (IAP), originally intended to fast-track development in districts that are severely affected by Maoist violence. Initially, there were 33 districts. But other backward and tribal districts were also added and the IAP now covers 82 districts. In a parallel kind of initiative, security-related expenditure (SRE) is largely borne by the Centre in 83 districts. What is interesting is that none of Gujarat's districts figure in the IAP or SRE lists. Nor does Gujarat find a mention in the list of states where there have been incidents of extremist violence. The Ministry of Home Affair's aforementioned Annual Report has several statements on what should be done to stem Naxalite violence. Some of these are directly police and security-related. In addition, "It is also necessary to simultaneously give focused attention to development and governance issues, particularly at the cutting edge level...Focused measures to ensure that the field and intermediate level functionaries of key departments such as health, education, drinking water, electricity, revenue and other development departments are available and accessible to the people. This would not only include filling up of posts/

3. The 17 per cent mentioned earlier is not a Census figure.

4. *http://censusindia.gov.in/Tables_Published/SCST/dh_st_gujarat.pdf*

5. Bibek Debroy and Laveesh Bhandari (ed.) (2003). *District-Level Deprivation in the New Millennium*. Delhi: Konark Publishers and Rajiv Gandhi Institute for Contemporary Studies.

6. *Annual Report* 2011-12, Ministry of Home Affairs.

vacancies, but also arrangements for their stay in the area of their posting. Identify critical infrastructure and development projects in the affected areas, as also critical infrastructure gaps, particularly in the sphere of connectivity, and formulate action plans to ensure the timely implementation of such projects. Create mechanisms for public grievance redressal, mass contact and public awareness, for creating an overall positive environment and confidence of the people in the local administrative machinery."[7]

Gujarat is geographically contiguous with Madhya Pradesh and Maharashtra, both states affected by extremist violence and districts like Panchmahals, Dohad, Vadodara, Narmada, Surat, Dangs, Navsari and Valsad are border districts too. With geographical proximity, negative spillovers are natural. If those spillovers have not happened, that is presumably because those developmental intentions mentioned by Ministry of Home Affairs have occurred in Gujarat and have not in other states. In similar vein, a paper was written about deprivation and its links with violence and conflict.[8] This said, "The raw data also showed that Naxalite-affected districts had higher poverty rates and low literacy rates than districts which were Naxalite-free. This time however, our econometric results showed that, even after controlling for other variables, the probability of a district being Naxalite-affected rose with an increase in its poverty rate and fell with a rise in its literacy rate. So, one prong in an anti-Naxalite strategy would be to address the twin issues of poverty and illiteracy in India." In other words, deprivation does not automatically lead to Naxalite-type violence, since that deprivation can be addressed. The fact that Gujarat has been able to contain such extremist activity is an achievement that is no less remarkable than the growth miracle.

What has Gujarat done that is different? The idea of TSPs (tribal area sub-plans) has been around since 1974, with financial allocations being made in proportion to shares of STs in total population, with a similar provision for SCs. However, in many instances and many states, these are just notional allocations in different line departments, though such funds are not meant to be diverted. When they are more than notional, they are frittered across a variety of schemes. The *Mid-Term Appraisal of the Eleventh Five Year Plan* stated this a little more politely. "Except for a few states, such as Tamil Nadu and Gujarat, the other states do not seem to be fixing realistic physical targets for SCSP and TSP schemes/programmes. Several states are not conducting benchmark surveys and also not preparing perspective plans and vision documents for long-term goals and outcomes of the schemes/programmes.

7. *Ibid.*

8. Borooah, Vani K. (2008). "Deprivation, Violence, and Conflict: An Analysis of Naxalite Activity in the Districts of India," *International Journal of Conflict and Violence* 2(2).

States, such as Andhra Pradesh, Maharashtra, Gujarat, Rajasthan, Orissa, Chhattisgarh, and Madhya Pradesh have adopted the practice of pooling funds from all the sectoral/line departments and placing them under the nodal Department of SC and ST Welfare. Preparation of SCSP and TSP documents earmarking funds in each Annual Plan as per the guidelines with prioritized schemes that benefit the SC and ST population is a prerequisite...Though the state governments are earmarking funds under SCSP and TSP as per the guidelines, the actual expenditure met under SCSP and TSP is typically way below the desired level of expenditure. State governments need to ensure full utilization of funds and also the intended benefits reaching the target groups in terms of measurable outcomes."[9] The first element in Gujarat was thus more efficient usage of TSP funds. The planning and budgetary powers were handed over to the Tribal Development Department.

In parallel with TSPs, the idea of ITDPs (Integrated Tribal Development Projects) has also been around for quite some time, with project administrators given some flexible funds for innovative schemes. As Table 8.1 shows, Gujarat has 12 such ITDPs.[10] Since 1997, discretionary funds have been given to every ITDP district. These are spent on programmes that cater to local needs, plugging gaps in existing schemes. They are thus based on decentralised planning. Chaired by the project administrator, Taluka Adijati Vikas Samitis have been constituted in *talukas* and schemes are approved and implemented by District Adjijati Vikas Mandals. Not only has this made expenditure more realistic, delinked from templates designed from above, the decentralisation has made the planning process more participatory and conveyed a sense of empowerment.

**Table 8.1**

*Integrated Tribal Development Projects*

| *Name of Project* | *District* | *Taluka/ Pocket/ Cluster* | *No. of Villages* | *Area Covered (sq km)* | *ST Population* | *% of Total Population* |
|---|---|---|---|---|---|---|
| 1 Khedbrahma | Sabarkantha | Khedbrahma | 137 | 846 | 153704 | 68.77 |
| | | Vijaynagar | 85 | 456 | 68545 | 75.62 |
| | | Bhiloda | 168 | 720 | 114007 | 55.30 |
| | | Meghraj | 129 | 545 | 51612 | 36.38 |
| | | Chorivad | 9 | 78 | 7062 | 40.84 |
| | | **Total** | **528** | **2645** | **394930** | **58.11** |

*contd...*

9. Planning Commission (2011). *Mid-Term Appraisal of the Eleventh Five Year Plan*. New Delhi: Government of India. *http://planningcommission.nic.in/plans/mta/11th_mta/MTA.html*

10. *http://guj-tribaldevelopment.gov.in/cms.aspx?content_id=4*

*...contd...*

| Name of Project | | District | Taluka/ Pocket/ Cluster | No. of Villages | Area Covered (sq km) | ST Population | % of Total Population |
|---|---|---|---|---|---|---|---|
| 2 | Dohad | Dohad | Dohad | 85 | 875 | 273469 | 74.21 |
| | | | Garhada | 34 | 257 | 134378 | 94.33 |
| | | | Jhalod | 151 | 798 | 319443 | 88.60 |
| | | | Fatepura | 96 | 302 | 170982 | 92.21 |
| | | | Limkheda | 152 | 1064 | 146764 | 61.32 |
| | | | Devgadhbaria | 91 | 1145 | 48185 | 23.14 |
| | | | Dhanpur | 90 | 466 | 89288 | 67.66 |
| | | | **Total** | **699** | **4907** | **1182509** | **72.26** |
| 3 | Godhra | Panchmahal | Santrampur | 162 | 1360 | 157852 | 72.07 |
| | | | Kadana | 136 | 428 | 80810 | 73.20 |
| | | | Ghoghamba | 95 | 747 | 72123 | 40.14 |
| | | | Mora(Godhra) | 31 | 194 | 50731 | 60.53 |
| | | | Kathola(Halol) | 61 | 224 | 34650 | 56.81 |
| | | | Govindi (Godhara) | 21 | 90 | 17451 | 53.81 |
| | | | Karoli(Kalol) | 3 | 29 | 7386 | 67.82 |
| | | | Jambughoda | 23 | 59 | 7816 | 56.94 |
| | | | **Total** | **532** | **3131** | **428819** | **60.03** |
| 4 | Chhotaudepur | Vadodara | Chhotaudepur | 145 | 768 | 175480 | 86.57 |
| | | | Naswadi | 217 | 535 | 107547 | 86 |
| | | | Kavant | 133 | 605 | 157738 | 92.50 |
| | | | Jetpur Pavi (Jabugam) | 211 | 806 | 175183 | 77.55 |
| | | | Vadali (Sankheda) | 53 | 172 | 26088 | 68.95 |
| | | | Bhatpur | 61 | 250 | 31125 | 56.29 |
| | | | **Total** | **820** | **3136** | **673161** | **82.39** |
| 5 | Rajpipla | Narmada | Dediapada | 214 | 1024 | 137553 | 95.81 |
| | | | Sagbara | 98 | 364 | 74980 | 89.65 |
| | | | Nandod | 204 | 1091 | 159443 | 68.98 |
| | | | Tilakwada | 97 | 245 | 29670 | 52.94 |
| | | | **Total** | **613** | **2724** | **401654** | **78.08** |
| 6 | Bharuch | Bharuch | Valia | 96 | 514 | 96179 | 73.65 |
| | | | Jhagadia | 168 | 813 | 115458 | 86.91 |
| | | | Ankleshwar | 38 | 226 | 36108 | 32.75 |
| | | | Amod (Mada Pocket) | 16 | 85 | 7643 | 54.09 |
| | | | Utraj(Hansot) | 13 | 92 | 6825 | 53.45 |
| | | | **Total** | **331** | **1730** | **262210** | **59.56** |

*contd...*

*...contd...*

| *Name of Project* | *District* | *Taluka/ Pocket/ Cluster* | *No. of Villages* | *Area Covered (sq km)* | *ST Population* | *% of Total Population* |
|---|---|---|---|---|---|---|
| 7 Songadh | Surat-I | Songadh | 179 | 1192 | 170464 | 88.45 |
| | | Uchchhal | 68 | 622 | 71084 | 97.32 |
| | | Vyara | 150 | 813 | 214011 | 84.71 |
| | | Valod | 40 | 202 | 64112 | 73.58 |
| | | Nizar | 87 | 396 | 83843 | 79.56 |
| | | **Total** | **524** | **3225** | **801114** | **83.53** |
| 8 Mandvi | Surat-II | Mandvi | 149 | 723 | 140800 | 75.74 |
| | | Mahuva | 69 | 354 | 112655 | 79.09 |
| | | Bandoli | 86 | 369 | 99213 | 47.07 |
| | | Mangrol | 94 | 511 | 90370 | 52.69 |
| | | Umarpada | 63 | 271 | 65867 | 96.45 |
| | | Kamrej | 60 | 308 | 52797 | 44.78 |
| | | Palsana | 43 | 170 | 38752 | 50.24 |
| | | Olpad | 38 | 177 | 21588 | 41.57 |
| | | Wanz (Choryasi) | 8 | 28 | 5291 | 40.08 |
| | | **Total** | **610** | **2911** | **627333** | **60.37** |
| 9 Vansada | Navsari | Vansada | 95 | 600 | 181785 | 90.31 |
| | | Chikhli | 92 | 575 | 205275 | 70.06 |
| | | Rahej(Gandevi) | 32 | 129 | 39630 | 56.83 |
| | | Sisidra Ganesh (Navsari) | 75 | 283 | 76989 | 42.38 |
| | | **Total** | **294** | **1587** | **503679** | **67.54** |
| 10 Valsad | Valsad | Dharampur | 106 | 713 | 165662 | 91.04 |
| | | Umargam | 51 | 361 | 115390 | 48.84 |
| | | Pardi | 82 | 426 | 158786 | 39.12 |
| | | Kaprada | 132 | 937 | 189939 | 93.63 |
| | | Atgam(Valsad) | 43 | 217 | 65482 | 52.09 |
| | | Ronvel | 30 | 157 | 47217 | 60.67 |
| | | **Total** | **444** | **2811** | **742478** | **60.42** |
| 11 Ahwa | Ahwa | Dangs | 311 | 1764 | 175079 | 93.76 |
| | | **Total** | **311** | **1764** | **175079** | **93.76** |
| 12 Palanpur | Banaskantha | Amirgadh (Palanpur) | 54 | 509 | 53808 | 53.21 |
| | | Danta | 124 | 562 | 91468 | 52.96 |
| | | **Total** | **178** | **1071** | **145276** | **52.92** |
| | | GRAND TOTAL | 5884 | 31642 | 6138245 | 68.23 |

This culminated in the VKY (Vanabandhu Kalyan Yojana), launched in 2007, together with the Eleventh Five Year Plan. VKY has 10 components, all designed to mainstream ITDP blocks on the road to development:



(1) Good quality and sustainable employment for five lakh tribal families, through agricultural productivity improvements, diversification into animal husbandry and dairy-based activities and skill training for tribal youth. For example, under the Wadi programme, wasteland has been productively used for orchards, mixed with vegetables. As has been mentioned earlier, four units of cattle have been provided, two through subsidies and two more through artificial insemination.

(2) Good quality higher education, with higher secondary schools that teach science in every *taluka*, Navodaya or Ekalavya type residential schools in each tribal *taluka*, establishment of colleges in remote and deprived *talukas*, new polytechnics and ITIs and scholarships and hostels.

(3) Accelerated economic development of tribal areas, through value addition in local natural resources, physical connectivity of remote tribal areas with roads, water supply, irrigation and power supply, and a specific financial allocation of Rs 1 crore for each *taluka*, to be used for developing clusters and links with markets.

(4) Health, through schemes like Chiranjeevi Yojana, financial assistance to BPL (below poverty line) families for surgeries, specific attention to malnutrition in pregnant and lactating mothers and under-six children and specific drives against endemic diseases like sickle cell anaemia and leptospirosis. For example, in tribal *talukas*, children in schools have been provided fortified and flavoured milk under the Sanjeevani Dudh programme.

(5) Housing for all ST families, with the idea that schemes like Indira Awas Yojana and Sardar Awas Yojana will be made for flexible and adapted to tribal lifestyles and preferences.

(6) Safe drinking water, with an eventual objective of providing piped drinking water.

(7) Irrigation, through group irrigation schemes, creation of water conservation structures on watershed basis, check-dams in tribal areas, subsidies, financial and technical assistance for oil engines and drip irrigation and drinking water cum irrigation projects.

(8) All-weather roads, with a focus on repairing and improving existing roads and covering all hamlets with population sizes of less than 250 with road networks.

(9) Universal electrification, through electrifying hamlets that have not so far been covered and ensuring free electrification to BPL families. If grid-based solutions are not possible, there will be off-grid solutions, such as through solar energy.

(10) Urban development, with all tribal *talukas* to be connected through broadband connectivity and 13 tribal towns to be developed as growth engines. Subsidised LPG (liquified petroleum gas) connections will be provided to BPL tribal families and fair-price shops in ITDP *talukas* upgraded.

It is true that some of these are still intentions and are in the pipelines. However, one can already see the changes, especially in agricultural diversification and dairy and animal husbandry, availability of water and electricity, better quality roads and schools and skills training. That indeed is the bottom line of this chapter. When does deprivation become discontentment that is violent? The answer has a dynamic rather than a static angle. When the deprivation is seen to be perpetuated and not seen to be progressively reduced, resentment is inevitable. But clearly, in Gujarat's tribal areas, this is not the case. It is not only the case that one's one life is getting better. One can perceptibly see that one's sons and daughters will lead better and less deprived lives. Had the Planning Commission's Expert Group authored the report in 2012, it would probably have approvingly referred to Gujarat, since Gujarat has practiced what the Expert Group preached. Over and above the broader growth and inclusion story, this is one aspect of the Gujarat model that States affected by extremist violence would do well to replicate.

# 9

# Governance

GUJARAT'S ECONOMY has often been written about. Rarely have people written about governance, at least directly. But without talking about governance, it is difficult to appreciate what has happened in the state.

The expression 'governance' has now become a buzzword. Everyone uses it, without necessarily defining it. At one level, we have a concept of corporate governance, related to efficient management of corporations. That too, has a link with economic development. However, when we normally link governance with economic development, we have in mind what should actually be called public governance, related to the act of governing. A distinction is also sometimes drawn between the state and the government, the former being more permanent, while the latter refers to the incumbent elected government. But clearly, governance is more than these formal institutions of government. It is also about decision making processes and about interactions between civil society and these formal institutions. Good governance will be characterised by predictability, transparency and accountability, while bad governance will be the opposite. And these days, one seeks to improve the public governance function through electronic governance or e-governance. Most poverty and deprivation can be interpreted as resulting from asymmetric access to information. Information technology can certainly be a powerful tool in reducing this asymmetric access to information. Having said this, it is not easy to define governance. In 1997, there was a Conference of Chief Ministers on Effective and Responsive Administration. The Action Plan, emerging from this Chief Minister's Conference, focussed on three areas where administrative law reform was important: (a) making administration accountable and citizen friendly; (b) ensuring transparency and right to information; and (c) tackling corruption and motivating the civil services. There was also a Central government identification of departments where the citizen interface is the most. This Central government categorisation mentioned public grievances (electricity, water, telephone, ration cards, sanitation, public transport, police), rural services (land records, BPL cards), police (FIR registration, lost and found, missing persons), social services (pensions, land acquisition, rehabilitation and compensation, registration of licenses and certificates, ration cards, birth certificates, death certificates, domicile certificates, caste/tribe certificates, arms renewal, registration of documents, motor vehicle registration, driving licenses, school registration, university registration), public information (employment exchanges, examination results, railway, road and airline timetables, government notifications, government forms, government schemes, hospital/bed availability and services), agriculture (information about seeds, pesticides, fertilisers, crop diseases, weather forecasts, market prices), utilities (electricity, water, telephones), commercial (taxation and

જૈવિક ખાતરનાં ઉપયોગથી
રસાયણીક ખાતર ખર્ચમાં ઘટાડો
એગ્રો જૈવિકા
પ્રવાહી જૈવિક ખાતર
એઝોટોબેક્ટર

return filing) and government (electronic procurement). The intention behind this identification was to increasingly resort to e-governance.

There is a link between bad governance and corruption too, though corruption has many dimensions. For our purposes, we are talking about corruption in the delivery of public goods and services. The *Approach Paper to the Twelfth Five Year Plan* has recently been finalised.[1] This states, "Poor governance leads to corruption, both petty and large, both of which corrode the moral fabric of the society. Large scale corruption occurs either because of mishandling of government contracts, or because discretionary decision making in some areas is used to the advantage of some. Corruption undermines the legitimacy of the system in the eyes of the public and reduces potential for achieving efficiency through competition...Corruption surfaces in many forms, all of which erode the confidence of the citizen in the quality of governance. They range from petty corruption associated with getting permissions that should be routinely available, large scale corruption associated with faulty procedures for handing large contracts and also corruption arising from discretionary decision making. ...However, public perception of corruption as a pervasive problem has increased. This is in part because of greater awareness and increased transparency (e.g., the Right to Information Act) and also the operation of a vigilant Press, especially the electronic media... We must aim at preventing corruption through further simplification of procedures for delivery of public services introducing greater transparency in public procurement processes. We must also strengthen mechanisms for dealing with corruption after it occurs through institutions such as the Lokpal and Lokayuktas...Corruption associated with government contracts can be minimized by restructuring government procurement processes." Corruption in such public service delivery is not distributionally neutral. It hurts the poor relatively more than the relatively rich. The poor can be a citizen. The poor can also be a self-employed person.

For such kinds of corruption, there is an oft-cited formula that has a lot of validity. Corruption = (Monopoly + Discretion) – (Accountability + Integrity + Transparency).[2] "The most cited causes of corruption include: (1) the absence of rules, regulations, policies and legislation; (2) weak systems of enforcement; (3) weak systems of oversight (i.e., the absence of a watchdog institution); (4) lack of accountability; (5) lack of transparency; (6) lack of checks and balances in the system (e.g., institutional weaknesses in the legislative and judicial systems); (7) lack of integrity; (8) monopoly of power; (9) high degree of discretion; (10) low salaries; (11) high rewards compared to risks; and (12)

1. Planning Commission (2001). *Faster, Sustainable and More Inclusive Growth: An Approach to the 12th Five Year Plan*. August.

2. UNDP (2008). *Primer on Corruption and Development*. December. *www.undp.org/governance*

low detection rate."[3] Therefore, the antidote to corruption also follows. First, there is an issue of reforming the civil services, including codes of conduct, salaries, entry and promotions and laws against corruption that are credible. Second, this implies the existence of independent anti-corruption bodies. Third, the monopoly in providing public services can be ended by enabling private sector delivery, since many such public goods and services are no longer instances of market failure. Fourth, public procurement needs to become much more transparent. Fifth, countervailing pressure must be created by civil society, which in turn, requires awareness and dissemination of information. This is a framework that is useful in understanding what has been accomplished in Gujarat.

E-governance is part of the answer, since it reduces the human interface. There have been several e-governance initiatives in Gujarat and e-governance has become functional in all municipalities and municipal corporations. There is an impressive list of e-governance awards.[4] Among the ones that have received such awards are e-Mamta, ICT (information and communication technology) solutions for planning and monitoring MGNREGS (Mahatama Gandhi National Rural Employment Guarantee Scheme) works, OASIS (online application and scrutiny of inter-state transactions), e-governance of mineral administration, e-governance initiatives and ICT initiatives in the Chief Minister's Office, online voting, e-dhara in the Revenue Department for computerisation of land records, SWAGAT (state-wide attention on grievances by application of technology) in the Chief Minister's Office, the IWMP (Integrated Watershed Management Programme), e-procurement by the Industry and Mines Department, VATIS (Value Added Tax Information System) in the office of commercial taxes, the HMIS (Hospital Management Information System) of the Health and Family Welfare Department, the IFMS (Integrated Financial Management System) in the Finance Department and ICT usage within the judiciary. A GSWAN (Gujarat state-wide area network) connects government offices, down to the level of *talukas*. The e-Gram Vishvagram project connects 13,716 *gram panchayats* and 6,000 common service centres. Other than this, for specific instances like Ahmedabad Municipal Corporation, there is an e-city project for delivering municipal services. While e-governance has G2C and G2B dimensions, one should not forget its G2G dimensions. The IWDMS (Integrated Workflow and Document Management System) and SICN (Sachivalaya Integrated Communication Network) have certainly improved budgetary and treasury functions.

On the corruption issue, corruption is perceived to be a crime. But there is no absolute definition of 'crime'. The Second Administrative Reforms

3. *Ibid.*

4. *http://www.gujaratinformatics.com/e_Governance_awards.html*

Commission (ARC) had a 4th report, titled *Ethics in Governance*.[5] This gives a useful summary of the history of India's laws against corruption. For the moment, it is sufficient to note that corruption is defined as public corruption, corruption committed by public servants, sometimes also referred to as bureaucratic corruption. Most discussions of corruption in the economic literature also define corruption in this sense.[6] Corruption in the private sector is increasingly regarded as an issue and perhaps India's laws will also eventually capture this. But that is not what the law is right now.

The National Crime Records Bureau brings out a 'Crime in India' database.[7] Chapter 9 of this document is on economic offences and has sections on cognisable crimes registered and disposed under PCA (Prevention of Corruption Act) and relevant sections of IPC (Indian Penal Code). Corruption related crimes are handled through various means. Not all are cognisable. Some are handled through departmental investigations. And there is quite a bit of inter-state variation, illustrated in Table 9.1.[8] The state-level variations are brought out with the help of an index constructed using data from 4 five year periods—1990-1995, 1996-2000, 2001-2005 and 2006-2010. Annual data were first aggregated for each of these periods and the following ratios were created: number of persons arrested out of every 1000 government employees; cases charge sheeted as a share of total cases investigated; cases sent for trial or departmental action as a share of those charge sheeted; proportion of cases that resulted in recoveries out of total cases investigated; proportion of cases that resulted in convictions as a share of trials; and proportion of persons who were finally charge sheeted as a share of those in custody or bail. These six ratios were normalised using the standard maxmin approach and then aggregated with equal weights. There are always problems with creating an index like this. With that qualification, Bihar and Gujarat stand out in anti-corruption efforts, with Gujarat improving from 2001. There are special anti-corruption courts in Ahmedabad and Surat.

Anti-corruption efforts cannot be delinked from speeding up the criminal justice system and swift dispute resolution is also part of any governance agenda. Data are slightly dated, since they go back to December 2007.[9] In that

5. Administrative Reforms Commission (2007). *Ethics in Governance*. 4th Report of 2nd Administrative Reforms Commission. January. *http://arc.gov.in/4threport.pdf*

6. For example, Bardhan, Pranab (1997). "Corruption and Development: A Review of Issues", *Journal of Economic Literature* 35 and Becker, G.S. and G.J. Stigler (1974). "Law Enforcement, Malfeasance, and Compensation of Enforcers", *Journal of Legal Studies* 3.

7. National Crime Records Bureau (NCRB) 2010. *Crime in India 2009*. Ministry of Home Affairs, *www.ncrb.nic.in*

8. The details of the index are given in Debroy, Bibek and Laveesh Bhandari (2011). *Corruption in India: The DNA and the RNA*. Konark Publishers.

9. Data come from different sources, though they all originate with the Ministry of Law, Justice & Company Affairs. Some data are from the *Annual Reports of the Ministry*, others from answers to Parliamentary questions and still others from the Supreme Court's online *Court News*.

**Table 9.1**

*Rating Major States on Anti-Corruption Efforts*

| States | 1990-1995 | 1996-2000 | 2001-2005 | 2006-2010 |
|---|---|---|---|---|
| Bihar | 0.41 | 0.30 | 0.43 | 0.88 |
| **Gujarat** | **0.48** | **0.57** | **0.64** | **0.69** |
| Andhra Pradesh | 0.53 | 0.73 | 0.55 | 0.61 |
| Punjab | 0.32 | 0.46 | 0.46 | 0.60 |
| Jammu & Kashmir | 0.13 | 0.32 | 0.17 | 0.40 |
| Haryana | 0.33 | 0.60 | 0.31 | 0.37 |
| Himachal Pradesh | 0.26 | 0.14 | 0.23 | 0.35 |
| Uttaranchal | . | . | 0.32 | 0.33 |
| Tamil Nadu | 0.19 | 0.20 | 0.24 | 0.29 |
| Madhya Pradesh | 0.23 | 0.22 | 0.31 | 0.29 |
| Karnataka | 0.24 | 0.19 | 0.20 | 0.29 |
| Rajasthan | 0.27 | 0.23 | 0.26 | 0.27 |
| Kerala | 0.16 | 0.20 | 0.22 | 0.27 |
| Maharashtra | 0.45 | 0.29 | 0.27 | 0.26 |
| Chhattisgarh | . | . | 0.34 | 0.24 |
| Uttar Pradesh | 0.11 | 0.11 | 0.16 | 0.21 |
| Orissa | 0.22 | 0.16 | 0.15 | 0.19 |
| Assam | 0.21 | 0.02 | 0.14 | 0.17 |
| Jharkhand | | 0.25 | 0.17 | |
| West Bengal | 0.11 | 0.08 | 0.03 | 0.01 |

year, Gujarat High Court had a pendency of 115,394, with a figure of 139,467 in December 2005. Most of these were civil cases. Therefore, at the High Court level, there has been some decline. In Gujarat's lower courts, there was a pendency of 2.42 million in 2007, a number that went down to 2.24 million in 2008. As is the pattern with other states, most of these lower court cases are criminal cases. There have been several pendency reduction attempts, not specific to Gujarat alone, such as Lok Adalats, Fast Track Courts (Gujarat has 166 of these), Family Courts (Gujarat has 7 of these), Mobile Courts, People's Courts, Women's Courts and video conferencing. Gujarat specific initiatives are evening courts (started in 2006), upgradation of infrastructure and new court complexes for lower courts, reduction in holidays, increase in court working hours, Labour Courts in Jamnagar and Mehsana, 6 special courts under the Vanbandhu Kalyan Yojana, Nari Adalats and pre-adjudication conciliation and mediation. While many criminal cases are IPC cases, several more are under SLL (special and local laws). A question should therefore be posed, especially for SLL. In an era of liberalisation, do all activities listed under SLLs need to be offences? And if they are offences, must they necessarily invoke criminal provisions, as opposed to civil ones? But these issues are outside the control of the Gujarat government, as are questions of filling judicial vacancies, necessary for reducing backlog. However, one should mention that the Gujarat Legal Services Authority has pushed for alternative methods of dispute resolution, including pre-litigation conciliation. Other than regular Lok Adalats, there have been mobile Lok Adalats too. On police reforms, unlike several states, Gujarat passed the amendment to the Bombay Police Act in 2007.

Let us return to public goods and services, such as electricity, water, sanitation, ration cards, public transport, licenses, certificates of different types, registration of different types, education, health, public information on government schemes and so on. Part of the problem is that people do not know about their entitlements. If citizens know about their rights, it is easier to exert countervailing pressure that such goods and services should be satisfactorily delivered. The first element of the governance plank has thus been one of making this information publicly available. There is the RTI (Right to Information) Act of 2005 and rules under RTI were notified in English and Gujarati in 2005. Using ITES and the e-governance idea, this information is available on the Internet, as is assorted information on government schemes, resolutions, circulars and forms. Moving a bit away from citizens, for tenders too, information is available on the Internet and e-procurement has been used. Returning to citizens, Citizen Charters have been published for 23 government departments and this goes down to the level of districts. E-governance based information on rights and entitlements does not get very far if IT usage is limited. But as mentioned earlier, GSWAN connects government offices, down to the level of talukas. Nor does awareness about rights and entitlements get very far on its own, unless there is a redressal mechanism. This is where SWAGAT in the Chief Minister's Office, kicks in. More often than not, grievances are settled the same day.

If awareness is the first plank of improved governance, elimination of discretion and monopoly is the second. In both education and health, instances have been given earlier of moving away from traditional government monopolies in delivery. All district offices have Jan Seva Kendras and there are civic centres too, in municipalities and municipal corporations. At these, assorted certificates (caste, domicile, residence, birth, death), affidavits, driving licences and ration cards are issued the same day. Under the e-gram project, some of these have also been taken down to *taluka* and *gram panchayats*, facilitated by computerisation of land records. There has been third party audit of such Jan Seva Kendras too.

The third element of improved governance is decentralisation and participatory planning and there is a feedback loop from citizens to government, to suggest ideas to the government. That principle of decentralised planning needs to be considered against the backdrop of the fact that Gujarat has a tradition of PRI (Panchayati Raj Institutions). The Gujarat Panchayat Act was enacted in 1961 and implemented in 1963, though it was subsequently overtaken by the Gujarat Panchayat Act of 1963. Therefore, Gujarat has an antecedent of capacity in *panchayats*, straddling the three tiers of district *panchayat, taluka panchayat* and village *panchayat*. A Gujarat Panchayat Services Selection Board also goes back to 1973. There are training institutes for PRIs in Junagadh, Bhavnagar, Vadodara, Patan, Surat and Gandhinagar. One can thus understand the success of decentralised planning, though the fact that decentralisation has been done needs to be appreciated. Administrative structures and buildings have been strengthened in *taluka* and district *panchayats* and a Rurban project has been started to improve physical, electronic and knowledge connectivity in *panchayats*. One of the best, but not the only, examples of decentralisation and participatory planning is in the water sector, where check-dams, farm ponds, village ponds and *boribundhs* were restored, or constructed, with the involvement of the community. There are also *pani samitis* through WASMO (Water and Sanitation Management Organisation), which was set up as a special purpose vehicle in 2002. *Pani samitis* are formed in *gram sabhas*, not just for water, but sanitation too. Out of 18,066 villages, 17,696 already have *pani samitis*. This should not be taken to mean that all *pani samitis* are equally advanced, since projects have only started in 3,923 of these villages. For some of the regional water supply schemes, social audits have also been held. Under WASMO, the community is involved in deciding what water supply is desired in a village and is also entrusted with the O&M (operation and maintenance) responsibility. The community needs to chip in with a 10 per cent capital cost before implementation is started. Other than operating the system and carrying out minor repairs, the community also sets norms for tariffs and distribution of water (time, duration, frequency), collects water tariffs and maintains records. There are a few *pani samitis* that are run only by women. In 2009, WASMO won a UN Public Service Award for innovative mechanisms that foster participation in decision making.

Fourth, the decentralisation has now gone down to the level of the *taluka*. The history of identifying backward *talukas* in Gujarat goes back to 1966.[10] That history, and the kind of indicators used for identification, is not very relevant for the present discussion. What is relevant is that there are 41 backward or 'developing' *talukas* now. Thirty (30) of these were identified

10. See, Government of Gujarat (2011). *Mid-Term Appraisal of State Flagship Scheme of Developing Talukas*. General Administration Department (Planning). November.

WASMO

in 2006 and another 11 were added in 2009. The 30 identified earlier are spread across the districts of Panchmahals, Banaskantha, Dohad, Vadodara, Tapi, Patan, Narmada, Kachchh and Surendranagar. The 11 now ones are in the districts of Surendranagar, Banaskantha, Bharuch, Tapi, Kuchchh, Bhavnagar and Panchmalas. Though the 41 are geographically spread out, there is a concentration in the north, the east and the south-east. Why are these *talukas* backward or developing? At an obvious level, that is because of the absence of public goods and services of different types. This is despite public expenditure, through Central government and state-specific schemes. For example, the Backward Regions Grant Fund covered the districts of Dohad, Banaskantha, Dangs, Narmada, Sabarkantha and Panchmahals. Since the Eleventh Five Year Plan (2007-2012), the Gujarat government has had a special focus on human development, including these 41 developing *talukas*. A bit of this is through additional state-specific programmes like the Vanabandhu Kalyan Yojana or the Sagarkhedu Yojana. But more importantly, there has been a decentralisation of planning, something that the 73rd and 74th Constitutional Amendments visualised. If one criticises centralised templates of CSSs (centrally sponsored schemes), that is no less true of templates designed in Gandhinagar. Accordingly, for these 41 developing *talukas*, Taluka Planning Committees are supposed to devise developmental plans and projects. The ATVT (Apno Taluko Vibrant Taluka) idea takes it down even further, to the sub-district level. Other than additional discretionary and development funds being available, there is the somewhat remarkable idea of assigning one of these 41 developing *talukas* to a senior civil service officer.

Fifth, that improved governance is also a function of altered mindsets in the bureaucracy, which received a clear focus after the rehabilitation work connected with the 2001 earthquake, was over. The Chintan Shibirs, annual retreats of ministers and senior bureaucrats, have been going on since 2003 and are illustrative. Other than the obvious synergies of such retreats, these ensured that government does not work in silos and departments and enabled cross-fertilisation of ideas. For example, the idea of each officer at district and *taluka* levels taking up an innovative project, without financial constraints, emerged through such a Chintan Shibir. Kanya Kelvani, Praveshotsava, Gunotsava, Krishi Melas and participation in *gram sabha* meetings are other instances of taking bureaucracy down to the grassroots. Better formulation of schemes, and better implementation, have resulted. Within government, there is a database of employees and suggestions for better governance have been invited from employees. Transfers, postings and implementation have become more insulated from political interference.

In cross-country governance surveys, there is a clear correlation between improved governance, however defined and measured, and economic development, however measured. The direction of causation is difficult to establish. Does better governance lead to economic development? Do higher levels of income and awareness trigger the demand for better governance? Or are their links that cut across both economic development and governance? That debate apart, in Gujarat's case, we clearly have better governance and higher levels of economic development, not just in terms of GSDP (gross state domestic product) growth, but improvements in other indicators too.

# 10

# Sectoral Issues

IN ANY DISCUSSION OF ANY COUNTRY or State's economy, it is customary to discuss sectoral compositions of GDP or GSDP early on—primary/agriculture, secondary/industry, tertiary/services etc. We have stayed away from that so far and one needs to plug the gap.

In popular perception, at least in some quarters, Gujarat's economic growth is about industry. Gujarat is about an investment destination for industries, about vibrant Gujarat. It is about sectors like biotech and pharmaceuticals, chemicals and petrochemicals, engineering, automobiles and ancillaries, food and agri-business, gas, oil and power, gems and jewellery and IT. Since 2003, the Vibrant Gujarat Summits have been held every two years, and the next one is scheduled for 2013. The Industrial Policy of 2009 mentioned clusters, industrial estates, industrial parks, IRs (investment regions) and SIRs (special investment regions) and we have spoken about these earlier. The Industrial Policy was fairly liberal. Industry does not mean only manufacturing. Other than manufacturing, electricity, gas, water supply and construction are also part of manufacturing. The Planning Commission gives annual average real rates of growth for industrial NSDP (net state domestic product). Between 2004-05 and 2008-09, this was 12.65 per cent for Gujarat, surpassed only by Chhattisgarh, Meghalaya, Orissa, Tripura, Andaman & Nicobar Islands and Puducherry.[1] As is the case with GSDP growth, a different time frame or a different method of constructing averages, will change the numbers, but will not alter the essential growth story. As has just been mentioned, this is not manufacturing alone. Shares in GSDP, or NSDP, depend not only on how industry has fared, but also on how the primary and tertiary sectors have done. In constant prices, industry's share in Gujarat's GSDP has increased from 36.5 per cent in 2004-05 to 39.4 per cent in 2010-11.[2] This is an increase, but perhaps not as much of an increase as one might have assumed *a priori*. That is because this is a relative share and sometimes, one does not realise that Gujarat is also a tertiary sector economy. For example, the tertiary sector contributed 44.0 per cent of GSDP in 2004-05 and this increased to 46.0 per cent in 2010-11. The largest segment of the tertiary sector was trade, hotels, restaurants, transport, storage and communications, accounting for 26.6 per cent of GSDP in 2010-11. The primary sector's share dropped from 19.5 per cent in 2004-05 to 14.6 per cent in 2010-11. Roughly half of what was dropped by the primary sector was picked up by the secondary sector and the tertiary sector picked up the remaining half.

Within industry, manufacturing's share in GSDP has been almost flat, inching up from 27.3 per cent in 2004-05 to 27.6 per cent in 2010-11. The

1. *http://planningcommission.nic.in/data/datatable/0904/tab_40.pdf*

2. Directorate of Economics and Statistics (2012). *Socio-Economic Review, 2011-12: Gujarat State*. Gandhinagar: Government of Gujarat. February.

increase in industry's share in GSDP is thus accounted for by electricity, gas, water supply and construction. Other than the special industrial 'enclaves', the DICs (District Industries Centres) provide a single-window clearance, through SWIFT (Single Window Industries Follow up Team). In the Vibrant Gujarat summits, 76 MoUs (Memorandum of Understanding) were signed in 2003, 226 in 2005, 363 in 2007, 3,346 in 2009 and 8,380 in 2011.[3] There is often a criticism surrounding these MoUs, the hype hypothesis so to speak. Yes, there have been MoUs. But how many of these have led to actual investment flows? While this is a legitimate question, at one level, it is also unfair, not just for Gujarat, but for any state. A MoU is only a preliminary step. Following that, there will be an EM (Entrepreneurship Memorandum) for a SME (small and medium enterprise), an IEM (Industrial Entrepreneurship Memorandum) for a non-SME project that is not subject to compulsory licensing and a LOI (letter of intent) for something that requires compulsory licensing. Assuming that registration of the firm is not required, land will have to be acquired or obtained. There will be environment, construction/building, water, power and indirect tax clearances. The financial requirements will have to be taken care of and only after all this is over, can the final clearance be obtained. In other words, no matter how fast the track is, there is a time lag. With that qualification, between August 1991 and March 2012, there were 11,517 approvals in Gujarat, covering IEMs, LOIs and EOUs.[4] This was 11.85 per cent of the all-India IEM number, 10.42 per cent of the all-India LOI number and 11.95 per cent of the all-India EOU number. However, these are numbers, not values. If one uses values instead, Gujarat had 11.22 per cent share of IEMs, a 20.06 per cent share of LOIs and a 3.68 per cent share of EOUs. *Ipso facto*, Gujarat's average LOI project had higher value, Gujarat's average EOU project had lower value and Gujarat's average IEM project had more or less the same value as the all-India average. More importantly, of the 11,517 projects since August 1991, 48.9 per cent had been implemented (employment generation of 960,000) and 28.2 per cent were under implementation (employment generation of 695,000).[5] That is not a bad strike rate. Those are in terms of numbers. If one uses values, of the Rs 10,695 billion worth of projects contemplated since August 1991, 18.4 per cent had been implemented and 68.1 per cent were under implementation. That's not too bad a strike rate either, especially if one includes those that are under implementation. Evidently and understandably, the time lag is longer for projects with larger value. Most of these projects are in sectors like metallurgy, industrial machinery, transport equipment, other engineering, electrical engineering

3. Ibid.

4. *http://ic.gujarat.gov.in/?page_id=846*. Data for 100% EOUs (export oriented units are till December 2003.)

5. Ibid.

and electronics, food processing, textiles, chemicals and petrochemicals, drugs and pharmaceuticals, glass, ceramic and cement and infrastructure. They are also concentrated in districts like Ahmedabad, Bharuch, Surat, Vadodara, Valsad, Gandhinagar, Rajkot and Kachchh. To set the perspective, Gujarat accunts for 7.2 per cent of India's GSDP, but 15 per cent of both India's industrial output and capital formation.

There are reasons why Gujarat is a favoured investment destination. There are generic constraints that plague industry and manufacturing and these have often been talked about.[6] A NMCC (National Manufacturing Competitiveness Council) was set up in 2005. In 2006, this produced a National Strategy for Manufacturing.[7] Barring infrastructure, the generic problems mentioned in this are indirect taxation, labour laws, procedural and administrative law, credit, skills and land problems. In 2000, the Prime Minister's Council on Trade and Industry also submitted a report on administrative and legal simplifications.[8] Understandably, this had an industry focus and listed the following as industry concerns. "Large number of clearances/permissions required; Complex regulation governing day to day functioning; Multiple agencies regulating operations functioning independently; Lack of co-ordination between various governing agencies; Frequent changes in policies/procedures/tariff structures; Unpredictability of changes; Lack of clarity on issues between Centre and States; Transaction oriented approach of the system instead of a corporate approach, leading to increased costs and delays; Lack of openness and transparency in communication and providing information." Fiscal incentives, say for textiles or salt, are increasingly irrelevant, or come low down the ladder, in determining the investment attractiveness of a state, some of those generic issues mentioned being outside the domain of state-specific policy. More important are issues like fast-tracked, simplified and streamlined procedures, law and order, physical infrastructure (particularly power and roads), social infrastructure (particularly skills), land availability and easier labour laws (procedural, if not statutory). It is on these that Gujarat scores. On labour laws, in 2006, TeamLease produced an *India Labour Report* that sought to rank States on the basis of their labour ecosystems, a combination of labour demand, labour supply and labour laws.[9] The details of the variables used and methodology do not really matter. What is important is that in the overall labour ecosystem,

6. Panagariya, Arvind (2008). *India: The Emerging Giant*. Oxford University Press. 2008; Planning Commission (2008). *Eleventh Five Year Plan, 2007-2012, Vol. III*. Government of India and Oxford University Press and CII-McKinsey (2004). *Made in India: The Next Big Manufacturing Export Story*. October. are examples.

7. *The National Strategy for Manufacturing*, 2006, *http://nmcc.nic.in/pdf/strategy_paper_0306.pdf*

8. This was chaired by Kumar Mangalam Birla.

9. *Labour Report 2006: A Ranking of Indian States by their Labour Ecosystem*. TeamLease Services.

the top three states were Delhi, Gujarat and Karnataka, in that order. We have already mentioned earlier that Gujarat has introduced self-certification and reduced the number of inspectors. Industrial disputes (strikes and lockouts) in Gujarat average around 20 a year.[10]

The trade union issue is a slightly problematic one. There are 11 central trade union organisations recognised by the Ministry of Labour, such recognition is contingent on the membership being spread over at least 4 states and total membership consisting of at least 500,000.[11] The verification data are extremely old and go back to 2002, exhibiting a total membership of 24.6 million, with BMS (Bhartiya Mazdor Sangh), INTUC (Indian National Trade Union Congress), HMS (Hind Mazdor Sabha), CITU (Centre of Indian Trade Union) and AITUC (All India Trade Union Congress) leading the membership tally, in that order. Unions are not necessarily those of workers, since there are employer unions too. It is important to remember this when considering data on registered unions. Out of the registered unions in 2002, 99.5 per cent (37,903) were of course unions of workers.[12] But only 20.4 per cent of these submitted returns, suggesting a reluctance to be transparent about membership. Of the 7,734 unions that submitted returns, 88.8 per cent were state-level unions, while the remainder consisted of Central Unions. Among Central Unions, the most members are in Tamil Nadu, followed by Gujarat. However, for state-level unions, the most members are in Gujarat, followed by Assam. In talking about unions, it is usually assumed that this is a manufacturing problem. This is a bit of a simplification. The likes of INTUC, AITUC, HMS, BMS and CITU have had traditional strengths and support bases in manufacturing. But the numbers suggest an erosion of that traditional support based, with an increased switch to services and the rural sector. Stated differently, within the union category, there has been a switch in importance from unions in the organised sector to unions in the unorganised sector. The importance of SEWA (Self-Employed Women's Association), which explains the high state-level membership in Gujarat, is a case in point.

Industry is not just about large scale industry. That is also a misconception. The Indian labour market is segmented. In a recent study, the World Bank stated, "Of the 413 million prime-aged persons in the Indian labour force in 2004-05, the overwhelming majority, about 90 per cent, are employed

10. Directorate of Economics and Statistics (2012). *Socio-Economic Review, 2011-12: Gujarat State.* Gandhinagar: Government of Gujarat, February.

11. These 11 are AICCTU, AITUC, AIUTUC, BMS, INTUC, INTTUC, CITU, HMS, LPF, SEWA, TUCC and UTUC. With the exception of SEWA, which is somewhat different, all the others are affiliated to political parties. However, this is only a list of those which are Centrally recognised. There are several others, without such Central recognition.

12. *Trade Unions in India 2002*. Labour Bureau.

in low productivity informal sector jobs."[13] The reference is to 2004-05, the 61st round of NSS (National Sample Survey), because NSS large samples are held at infrequent intervals, with an average gap of five years in between. The results of the next large sample (66th round, 2009-10) have not been analysed. Consequently, most data based work is still based on 2004-05 numbers. The NCEUS (National Commission for Enterprises in the Unorganised Sector) was set up in 2004 and one of its reports had a very good discussion of definitional and statistical issues in analysing India's informal economy.[14] For our purposes, let us use the terms organised and formal synonymously, just as the terms unorganised and informal are used synonymously. In contrast with developed economies, and also in contrast with several developing economies, a large chunk of employment occurs in the rural sector. Outside of agriculture, informality can be defined in one of three different ways. First, there is a definition in terms of exemptions from paying indirect taxes. Second, there is a definition in terms of SSI (small scale industry), which again is defined in terms of threshold levels of investment in plant and machinery. Third, there is a definition in terms of labour laws. That is, an enterprise is unorganised if it uses power and employs fewer than 10 people or does not use power and employs fewer than 20 people.[15] Informal employment includes both self-employment in informal (small and unregistered) enterprises and wage employment in informal jobs (without labour contracts, worker benefits and protection). Typically, own account enterprises are not registered. In 2004-05, 84.9 per cent of own account enterprises were not registered and this needs to be flagged, because registration also brings attendant benefits, such as access to credit or government subsidies on marketing and technology. Why are not own account enterprises registered? The answer is not entirely lack of information. Opting out of registration is probably a conscious decision, because the benefits from registration are not commensurate with the costs. Not only are procedures connected with registration complicated and tiresome, registration brings with it the attendant problem of bribery and rent-seeking from the government machinery. The non-registration issue spills over into the existence of the unorganised sector in general. It is often presumed that rigid labour laws in the organised sector encourage informality. But this is a partial explanation. There are other reasons behind informality—avoidance of taxes, complicated transaction costs associated with registration, rent-seeking and few perceived benefits from formalisation. The Third SSI Census was held in 2000-01 and found that there were a large

13. World Bank (2010). *India's Employment Challenge: Creating Jobs, Helping Workers*. Oxford University Press.

14. NCEUS (2007). *Report on Conditions of Work and Promotion of Livelihoods in the Unorganized Sector. http://nceuis.nic.in/Condition_of_workers_sep_2007.pdf*

15. Strictly speaking, this is a Factories Act definition.

number of unregistered units in Gujarat too. When asked about the reasons for non-registration, 53.13 per cent said that they were not aware of the provisions, while another 39.8 per cent said that they 'were not interested'.[16] Those are results from the Third Census. We will turn to the results of the Fourth Census in a moment.

To return to the point about industry not being large scale industry alone, the 2009-10 survey of the ASI (Annual Survey of Industries) covered the entire factory sector. This shows an increase in the number of factories to 15,576 and 9.8 per cent of India's factories are in Gujarat.[17] At 13.22 per cent, the share is higher in net value added. In decreasing order of importance, these factories are in segments like chemical and chemical products, basic metals, machinery and equipment, non-metallic mineral products, textiles, food products and pharmaceuticals. Together, they provided employment of 1.2 million. Provisional figures show an increase in the number of factories to 25,206 in 2010, with an employment of 1.3 million. The number of factories has increased and so has the average employment per factory, from 748 in 1990 to 1,318 in 2010. After the MSMED (Micro, Small and Medium Enterprises) Act of 2006, the SSI Census became a MSME Census, conducted in 2006-07. This showed that Gujarat accounted for 14.70 per cent of the country's registered and working MSME enterprises and also accounted for 7.04 per cent of the country's registered and closed MSME enterprises.[18] This is a total of 0.23 million registered and working MSME enterprises in Gujarat. More interestingly, 0.13 million MSME enterprises in Gujarat were in 369 clusters, a pattern also exhibited in Tamil Nadu and Uttar Pradesh, cluster being defined as a concentration in manufacture of the same product group. This suggests that the positive externalities of cluster formation have tended to work and in all probability, many of these MSME enterprises perform an ancillary function. Also interestingly, as Table 10.1 shows, at least for SSI, there has been a sharp increase in the number of registered units.[19] Earlier, non-registration was described as a conscious choice, not just because of lack of information. Therefore, it is plausible to presume that transaction costs associated with registration having declined, there are greater benefits associated with registration and the tax enforcement machinery has also improved. Table 10.2 shows variation in SSI registration across districts.[20] Understandably, most SSI registration has been in relatively more advanced districts.

16. *http://dcmsme.gov.in/ssiindia/census/highlights.htm*

17. Directorate of Economics and Statistics (2012). *Socio-Economic Review, 2011-12: Gujarat State*. Gandhinagar: Government of Gujarat. February.

18. *http://www.dcmsme.gov.in/publications/FinalReport010711.pdf*

19. *http://ic.gujarat.gov.in/?page_id=855*

20. Ibid.

**Table 10.1**

*SSI Registration (in numbers): Year-wise*

| | |
|---|---|
| 1961 | 2169 |
| 1970 | 15849 |
| 1980 | 43712 |
| 1990 | 115384 |
| 1995 | 178627 |
| 2000 | 251088 |
| 2001 | 264668 |
| 2002 | 274315 |
| 2003 | 286185 |
| 2004 | 296306 |
| 2005 | 306646 |

**Table 10.2**

*SSI Registration (in numbers): District-wise*

| *District* | *Till 31 September 2006* |
|---|---|
| Ahmedabad | 65763 |
| Amreli | 4890 |
| Banaskantha | 6819 |
| Bharuch | 14328 |
| Bhavnagar | 11821 |
| Gandhinagar | 4808 |
| Jamnagar | 13236 |
| Junagadh | 7986 |
| Kheda | 13521 |
| Kutch | 6109 |
| Mehsana | 14602 |
| Panchmahals | 6704 |
| Rajkot | 32461 |
| Sabarkantha | 8601 |
| Surat | 47404 |
| Surendranagar | 8609 |
| Vadodara | 18498 |
| Valsad | 15966 |
| Dang | 53 |
| Anand | 2298 |
| Dohad | 1092 |
| Narmada | 816 |
| Navsari | 3357 |
| Patan | 2274 |
| Porbandar | 766 |
| | 312782 |

At the lower end of the industrialisation spectrum are cottage and rural industries. There are cluster development schemes for *khadi*, handlooms, handicrafts and skill upgradation and market development schemes. Other than schemes like Sagar Khedu Yojana, Vanbandu Kalyan Yojana, Garib Samruddhi Yojana and even Garib Kalyan Melas, something like Mission Mangalam is also an attempt to integrate animal husbandry, agro processing, food processing, aquaculture, processing of forest products, handlooms, handicrafts, garments, bamboo and timber products into markets, through Sakhi Mandals, SHGs (self-help groups) and other communities of the poor. GLPC (Gujarat Livelihood Promotion Company) Limited was set up in 2010 to implement Mission Mangalam. Part of this inclusion is a financial inclusion agenda.

There is a reason for mentioning this. In national income accounts, there is a simple classification of sectors into primary, secondary and tertiary.[21] But there is a broader definition of agriculture too and it is not that delinked from industry. Apart from anything else, there are sectors like inputs (seeds, fertilisers, agrochemicals, biotechnology), processing, storage, trade and distribution issues. These are secondary and tertiary sector issues. Development is correlated with a reduction in the number of people who are employed in agriculture. In relatively richer parts of the world, people have been pulled out of agriculture and into more productive activities. Indeed, there are several different types of movements that happen. People who remain in agriculture move away from producing foodgrains to other forms of crop output, such as horticulture. There is commercialisation and diversification. Others move away to allied activities like aquaculture, dairy-farming, floriculture and poultry. Still others move away from farm activities entirely to non-farm activities, such as rural industry and services. Therefore, once agriculture develops, it does not necessarily lead to an increase in the share of agriculture in GSDP. Instead, there are increases in the share of the secondary sector (processing say) and the share of the tertiary sector (transportation say).

Gujarat is known as a state with a strong manufacturing base and in constant prices, the primary sector's share in GSDP has declined from 19.5 per cent in 2004-05 to 14.6 per cent in 2010-11, a decline that was mentioned before.[22] Agriculture's share (this includes animal husbandry) has declined from 13.2 per cent in 2004-05 to 10.9 per cent in 2010-11. While the share has declined,

21. It is worth bearing this in mind when one considers figures like shares of agriculture in GDP or shares of population employed in agriculture. These may be declining, even in developing countries. However, interpreted in the broad sense of an agricultural supply chain that extends from the farm to the fork, the importance of food and agriculture does not decline commensurately.

22. Directorate of Economics and Statistics (2012). *Socio-Economic Review, 2011-12: Gujarat State*. Gandhinagar: Government of Gujarat. February.

the growth rate of Gujarat's agriculture, especially since 2000, has been remarkable and has been commented upon.[23] Between 2001 and 2012, the agricultural component in Gujarat's GSDP has grown at a real average rate of annual growth of 10.5 per cent, nothing short of remarkable. "Cotton, the high value segment (livestock, fruits and vegetables) and wheat are identified as the main sources of growth as they have grown rapidly both in production and value terms. Private sector has driven the cotton boom; but public sector has also played an important role. Besides favorable monsoons in the past few years and past investment in rural roads, active role of public sector through [a] mass based water harvesting and groundwater recharge; [b] reform of rural power system through Jyotigram Scheme; [c] reform of agricultural marketing institutions; [d] revitalized and reinvented agricultural extension system are among the factors that have contributed to Gujarat's impressive performance in agriculture."[24] The moral of the Gujarat story thus is—rural roads, water harvesting and groundwater recharge, rural power, agricultural marketing and extension services can drive high rates of growth. "Gujarat has slowly followed suit as it one of the few states to have implemented reforms to the Model Act 2003 and all amendments to the Agricultural Produce Marketing Committee (APMC) Act in 2007 allowing direct marketing, contract farming and markets in private/co-operative sectors...But be it a cooperative or private-sector led model, linking farmers to markets is crucial to promote agricultural growth and raise farmers' incomes...The corporate sector can play an important role by setting up back end operations like rural service hubs which supply inputs and extension services to farmers...Farmers can also come together in farmers cooperatives, companies or clubs to reduce the transaction cost of doing business and also correct the balance of power within the stakeholders (organized retailers, processors and farmers) in negotiating the terms of doing business...The state government has also worked with various institutions like state agricultural universities, NGOs/civil society organizations and companies in bridging the knowledge gap i.e. making agricultural technology and know-how available to farmers."[25]

To the above list, one can add a few other items not directly mentioned in the quotes. The Krushi Mahotsav programme was started in 2005 and is a month-long mass contact programme with farmers, including mobile 'Krushi Raths'. Soil health cards are issued for every plot of land and this enables optimum input usage and crop management. The Gujarat Cooperatives and Water Users Participatory Irrigation Management Act was passed in 2007

23. Gulati, Ashok, Tushaar Shah and Ganga Sreedhar (2009). *Agriculture Performance in Gujarat Since 2000*. International Water Management Institute and International Food Policy Research Institute. May.

24. Ibid.

25. Ibid.

and participatory irrigation management introduced. Through the Sardar Patel Participatory Water Conservation Scheme, check dams are built with monetary contribution from beneficiaries, 20 per cent in some cases and 10 per cent in others. Animal health camps have been organised in several villages. The upshot has been agricultural diversification, higher productivity and growth. A few numbers will illustrate the point. Irrigated area as a percentage of gross irrigated area has increased from 31.84 per cent in 2000-2001 to 44.71 per cent in 2006-07. From 1999-2000 to 2010-11, productivity (in kg/ha) has increased from 1,245 to 2,328 for cereals, from 563 to 812 for pulses and from 226 to 637 for cotton. However, yield increases have not been that marked for oilseeds and tobacco. Pumps used in irrigation and tractors used in agriculture have increased sharply, while the number of ploughs has stagnated. An IDDP (Integrated Dairy Development Project) was started in 2007 for BPL (below poverty line) ST families, to provide four heads of cattle for such households. Two heads of cattle are provided through a combination of a subsidy and a loan and two others through artificial insemination. The project has been implemented in the districts of Vadodara, Banaskantha, Panchmahal, Dohad, Valsad, Navasari, Dangs, Sabarkantha, Songadh, Mandvi, Narmada, Surat and Tapi, with district-level milk cooperatives and NGOs (non-governmental organisations) providing collection centres

RAW MILK SILO-4

and chilling facilities. Loan recovery has been high and per house, average monthly income from this enterprise is between Rs 3,000 and Rs 3,700. Of more recent vintage has been the IWADP (Integrated Wadi and Agriculture Diversification Project), started in 2009, though its pilot antecedents date to 2007. Interestingly, IWADP requires a participating entry free from BPL ST families who wish to participate. IWADP has two distinct strands. There is Project Sunshine strand for the dryland regions of north and central Gujarat, where one tries to push crops like hybrid maize, potato, mustard, pigeon pea and Bt cotton in districts like Sabarkantha, Banaskantha, Panchmahal, Dohad and Vadodara. And there are Jeevika projects for water-intensive areas in south Gujarat, where one tries to push vegetables like tomato, bitter gourd, bottle gourd, okra, pointed gourd, *parwal* and turmeric and fruits like mango, banana, cashew in districts like Narmada, Valsad, Tapi, Navsari, Surat and Dangs.

As one travels through Gujarat, there are examples of innovations in agriculture, involving NGOs, with instances of what can broadly be called PPPs (public private partnerships). Instead of individual purchases of tractors, tractor markets have been opened up, with tractors owned by a group through subsidies and offered on time sharing basis to others. The use of nets has reduced crop damage resulting from pests and insects and had also reduced the demand for irrigation water. However, integrating agriculture is not just about input markets and increasing productivity. It is also about accessing markets. That requires connectivity. This is probably the reason why the Jeevika projects have been more successful than Sunshine, so far.

The NAAS (National Academy of Agricultural Sciences) has just produced a report on the state of India's agriculture, for the year 2011-12.[26] This is an extremely good report, which documents not just the state of agriculture, but requisite reforms. There is an agricultural reform agenda and there is a rural reform agenda that goes beyond agriculture. Within the agriculture set, there are issues like allowing corporate sector involvement in agriculture, removal of government imposed restrictions on production, marketing and distribution,[27] refocus of public expenditure away from input subsidies to infrastructure[28] and extension services,[29] disintermediation of distribution

26. *http://www.indiawaterportal.org/sites/indiawaterportal.org/files/state-of-indian-agriculture-report-naas-2011-2012.pdf*

27. For instance, the Agricultural Produce Marketing and Control (APMC) Acts and orders under the Essential Commodities Act.

28. Plus decentralisation in the management of rural infrastructure.

29. There is also a research and development agenda, but it is not necessarily obvious why this has to be public sector driven. Extension services will have to be largely public sector driven.

chains, forward markets, contract farming, revamping credit and insurance, and freeing up of land markets.[30] All these are linked to encouraging commercialisation and diversification. There is also an issue of encouraging off-farm employment and this is where rural sector reforms kick in, through provision of physical and social infrastructure. Had these reforms actually been introduced, one would not have needed MGNREGS (Mahatama Gandhi National Rural Employment Guarantee Scheme) today. Indeed, if there is less demand for MGNREGS in a state, that is a positive sign, in the sense that the state is doing well in the rural sector.

A Commission on Centre-State Relations was set up and submitted a report in 2010.[31] One of the sub-reports focussed on the lack of a harmonised domestic market in agricultural products. This highlights the high compliance costs and the fragmentation of markets, leading to lack of economies of scale. The sub-report has the following kind of numbers from unification and harmonisation of agricultural markets.

- Reduction of post-harvest losses by 5-7 per cent for food grains and 25-30 per cent for fruits and vegetables.
- Static gains of 10 per cent through harmonising standards of agricultural products.
- Static efficiency gains of up to 20 per cent because of disintermediation of distribution chains, resulting in higher prices for farmers and lower prices paid by consumers. The welfare gains are roughly distributed in a ratio of 40 per cent for farmers (producers) and 60 per cent for consumers.
- Savings in compliance costs by 5 per cent consequent to fiscal unification.
- Reduction in transportation costs by 30 per cent.
- Incremental growth in agriculture & allied activities by 2 per cent because of static gains alone.
- Static increment to GDP growth by 1 per cent because of removal of interstate barriers alone. Increment by 2 per cent if broader agricultural cum rural sector reforms are undertaken.

30. There are two distinct issues of ownership laws and tenancy laws here. The former is contentious, the latter less so.

31. *http://interstatecouncil.nic.in/ccsr_report_2010.htm*

- Additional direct employment generation by 5 million a year. If one includes indirect employment, additional employment generation by 12 million a year.

One can quibble about the modelling used or the specific numbers in this sub-report. But the broad thrust remains. And while several of these are issues that concern the centre, it is probably true that some of these efficiency gains have been reaped in Gujarat's agriculture. This sectoral chapter suggests that Gujarat's growth is not just about high-profile vibrant Gujarat and large scale industry. It is also about the smaller end of the industrial continuum and an agricultural transformation that integrates into this process. But as with the social sector successes, some of these interventions date from the Eleventh Five Year Plan (2007-2012). And therefore, their effects and the consequent improvements in standards of living are not yet recognised.

# 11

# The Environment and Sustainable Development

THE EXPRESSION 'sustainable development' is a bit of a buzzword, though it is not always easy to pin it down. However one defines it, and this includes the 1987 Brundtland Report, sustainable development is about ensuring the needs of the present generation, without compromising on the needs of the future generation. If the consumption of renewable natural resources is more than nature's capacity to replenish them, any development is not sustainable. There are reasons why the environment and sustainable development are often not factored into standard GDP calculations.

The GDP for any economy or country is the total value of goods and services produced in the country over a designated time period, the time period usually being one year. This is a standard definition, one that can be found in any undergraduate economics text book. The problems with GDP measures also follow. First, GDP is an aggregate or summary measure and therefore, ignores the distribution. This is a characteristic of any measure that is in the nature of an average. Second, GDP is the value of goods and services that are produced. Valuation needs prices and prices need markets. Therefore, tautologically, GDP can only reflect goods and services that are marketable and have markets. Consequently, transactions that do not have markets cannot conceivably be captured in GDP. Examples are non-market transactions like unpaid work,[1] the non-monetised or underground economy and positive or negative externalities, environmental degradation being an instance of the latter. For instance, costs of global warming will not normally be factored into any GDP calculations. Simon Kuznets won the Nobel Prize in Economics in 1971 and is remembered for his pioneering work on US national income, measuring GDP (or gross national income) and economic development. In 1934, Simon Kuznets played a major role in drafting a report for the Senate on US national income between 1929 and 1932. As the following quote illustrates, the present criticisms of GDP were anticipated several decades ago.[2] "With quantitative measurements, especially the definiteness of the result suggests, often misleadingly, a precision and simplicity in the outlines of the object measured. Measurements of national income are subject to this type of illusion and resulting abuse, especially since they deal with matters that are the center of conflict of opposing social groups where the effectiveness of an argument is often contingent upon oversimplification...These constitute highly valuable uses of national income measurements, but only if the results are interpreted with a full realization of the definition of national income assumed, either explicitly or implicitly, by the measurement. Thus, the estimates submitted in the present study define income in such a way as

1. Domestic work by family members is an instance of this.

2. *http://library.bea.gov/cdm4/document.php?CISOROOT=/SOD&CISOPTR=888*, especially Chapter 1 on concept, scope and method.

to cover primarily only efforts whose results appear on the market place of our economy... All these qualifications upon estimates of national income as an index of productivity are just as important when income measurements are interpreted from the point of view of economic welfare...The welfare of a nation, can, therefore, scarcely be inferred from a measurement of national income as defined above." In the context of sustainable development and the environment, the problem is non-existence of markets, or more accurately, market failure. Marginal private costs are different from marginal social costs. Marginal private benefits are different from marginal social benefits. This is compounded by problems of information asymmetry.

Protecting the environment is indeed important and environmental degradation can also have disproportionate negative effects on the lives of the poor. However, here is a quote from the Eleventh Five Year Plan (2007-2012) document.[3] "The serious consequences of climate change, including especially the consequences for India, lead naturally to the question of what should be our response. Two types of responses need to be considered. The first relates to adaptation, i.e., measures that have to be taken given the very high likelihood that climate change will occur and will have adverse effects. The second relates to mitigation, i.e., steps to be taken that might reduce the extent of climate change. Since a substantial adverse change in climate appears unavoidable even with the optimal mitigation response, the process of adaptation to climate change must have priority. The most important adaptation measure is development itself. A stronger economy is more able to adapt both in terms of the cost of adaptation and technological capability. Achieving rapid economic growth as targeted in the Eleventh Plan is therefore a key element in adaptation....Recognizing the need for international co-operation in devising an effective mitigation strategy, in 1992, the international community established the UNFCCC which established the principle of 'common but differentiated responsibility' between the industrialized countries (Annex 1 countries) and the developing countries (non-Annex 1 countries), taking account of the respective capacities...An optimum approach to mitigation from a global perspective is only possible if all countries cooperate to facilitate collective action...The challenge lies in determining a basis for collective action which is fair, provides equitable entitlement to the global environment space with burden sharing in a manner which recognizes the very different levels of development and also the very different degrees of historical responsibility for causing the problem in the first place." Though the language used is different, this effectively says that, at low levels of economic development, the priority is growth and ensuring sustainable development is not without costs, sometimes in the form of lower growth.

3. *http://planningcommission.nic.in/plans/planrel/fiveyr/11th/11_v1/11th_vol1.pdf*

For the environment, a Kuznets curve is sometimes postulated. This simply means that, as economic development occurs, the environment degrades. When economic development crosses a certain threshold, measured say by per capita income, greater attention is paid to the environment and indicators tend to improve. In other words, the relationship is in the form of an inverse-U. The empirical evidence for this relationship is often debated. It seems to work better for water and air pollution, less well for other measures of environmental protection. Without getting into details of that debate, Gujarat's per capita income is roughly equal to the all-India average. With compulsions of growth and urbanisation, one would have expected the state's environmental indicators to be worse than they are, and for the environment to be less of a priority. Even for interesting is what empirical studies tend to find on the links between deforestation and economic development. Cross-country, the threshold there is something like 5000 US dollars and Gujarat is far short of that. Contrast that with the following quote. "Gujarat is one State which is already getting on with implementing initiatives to transform itself into a low carbon economy and is making real changes. Building on a model of positive partnerships between people, businesses, scientific community and government, the State has shown real commitment. The fact that the Government has gone ahead and set up its own full fledged department of Climate Change, is a clear declaration of intent and shows that the actions have been well-planned and thought through."[4] In terms of the Kuznets curve, Gujarat is thus ahead of the curve. "Some Indian states, including the Himalayan states, Gujarat, Kerala and Delhi have been proactive in addressing climate change." [5]

That department of climate change was set up in 2009 and its priorities are—the promotion of green technologies and funding research in this, the earning of more carbon credits, power saving, the preservation of groundwater, promotion of CNG (compressed natural gas) networks, the increase of mangrove cover, the preparation of a multidimensional climate change policy, introducing curricula on climate change in educational institutes and creation of public awareness. Consider this. Despite the emphasis on industrialisation, refineries and port-led development, there have been no major environmental disasters in Gujarat, along the coast, or elsewhere. Established in 2010, the SICOM (Society of Integrated Coastal Management) has implemented an ICZM (Integrated Coastal Zone Management) project in the Gulf of Kachchh, together with two other such projects in Odisha and West Bengal.

4. Howard, Steve (2011). "Foreword," in *Convenient Action, Gujarat's Response to Challenges of Climate Change*. Macmillan.

5. This is a quote from the Central Ministry of Environment and Forest (2011). *Sustainable Development in India: Stocktaking in the run up to Rio+20*. Government of India. *http://envfor.nic.in/downloads/public-information/Sust_Dev_Stocktaking.pdf*

There are several dimensions to protecting the environment—water, air, waste, forests, wildlife, and so on.[6] Institutionally, the Forests and Environment Department has four executing agencies the GPCB (Gujarat Pollution Control Board), the GEC (Gujarat Ecology Commission), the GIDE (Gujarat Institute of Desert Ecology) and the GEMI (Gujarat Environmental Management Institute).



GPCB has draft action plans for critically polluted areas like Ankleshwar, Vapi, Ahmedabad, Vatva, Bhavnagar and Junagadh. There has been an emphasis on cleaner production technologies in industries like dye and dye intermediates, chemicals and petrochemicals, pharmaceuticals, textiles, food and agro-based industries, fisheries and pulp and paper products. Defaulting industrial units have been served closure notices. CETPs (Common effluent treatment plants), STPs (sewage treatment plants), TSDFs (Common Hazardous Waste Treatment, Stabilisation and Disposal Facilities), CBMWTFs (Common Biomedical Waste Treatment, Stabilisation and Disposal Facilities) and common incinerators have been set up. Twenty-two (22) illegal hazardous dumping sites were identified and hazardous waste there shifted to TSDFs. The 2009 Industrial Policy includes environment management as part of infrastructure development and provides for these being developed on PPP (public private partnership) basis in new industrial estates. Municipal townships and colonies also have sewage treatment plants. Municipal waste is treated and disposed of through common secured landfills and Gujarat Urban Development Company Limited creates the infrastructure for treatment, transportation and disposal. There are several CDM (Clean Development Mechanism) projects, with CER (certified emission reduction) norms. Thirty-nine (39) of these, in sectors like energy and petrochemicals, urban transportation, forests and environment, rural development, industries and mines, are estimated to lead to certified emission reductions of 28 million per year. Data are available till 2009 and around 40 per cent of India's CDM market was in Gujarat.

In 2012, Planning Commission undertook a study on successful models of implementation of environmental policies and programmes in states.[7] On process re-engineering, this states, "Gujarat has provided incentives for objective and honest third party audit of environmental statements. The key elements of modified process seem to be less reliance on human involvement, collaboration with other agencies and industry, and integrating ICT with logical checks/intervention by the department." On use of ICT (information

6. We have glossed over noise pollution, which is also monitored.

7. Planning Commission (2002). *Successful Models of Implementation of Environmental Policies and Programmes in States*. May 7. *http://www.planningcommission.gov.in/reports/sereport/ser/successful_models09072012.pdf*

and cummunication technology) and technology, "GPCB developed web-based software application–XGN–for the day to day operations. Besides the primary use for consent management, it has e-communication through SMS, e-Talk, e-Message Box and Alerts. Queries in the form of SMS & immediate replies results in speedier disposals. XGN enables legal actions like show cause notices, closure directions & revocation orders. It also facilitates online payment of consent fees and Water Cess. Revenue of GPCB increased from 28 crore to 76 crore in the first two years of operation. The programme is a recipient of the National e-governance Award 2010 for Re-Engineering of Processes. This system has been replicated and being used by other states including HP, Uttaranchal, Goa, Andhra Pradesh and Madhya Pradesh." On third party outsourcing, "GPCB also has a third party monitoring scheme for industrial effluent quality monitoring. Gujarat also has third-party environmental audit scheme, wherein industries from the most polluting sectors must retain an approved auditor to report pollution readings to the GPCB and to recommend improvements to industry practices. This scheme is in addition to the regular GPCB inspection system. To strengthen this scheme and make it more transparent GPCB implemented a pilot that modified the scheme so that the auditors were paid from a central pool, rather than directly by the firms, and randomly assigned to each industry, rather than being chosen by the industry. Back-checks by independent local technical university were also done." On single window clearances, "The Andhra Pradesh Industrial single window clearance Act, 2002 came into effect from 2002. Similar facility is made available by Government of Maharashtra and Gujarat. Single window clearance has resulted in ease of application as well as speedier processing of applications (mainly due to their completeness) by State PCBs." Finally, "India is to launch its first emissions trading scheme (ETS), an air-pollution reduction pilot programme in three States that may go national in future. The industrial States of Tamil Nadu, Gujarat and Maharashtra volunteered to take part in the scheme, which was officially launched by the Ministry of Environment and Forests on 23 March, 2011."

There are plans for controlling air pollution in seven cities and there is an ambient air quality monitoring programme for Ahmedabad, Vadodara, Surat, Vapi, Bharuch and Rajkot. Table 11.1 shows the kind of data this monitoring throws up.[8] Table 11.1 does not quite show a clear trend, compounded by the problem that such data are counterfactuals. That is, one does not know what the figures would have been like, in the absence of interventions.

8. Collated from GPCB annual reports.

**Table 11.1**

*Ambient Air Quality, Ahmedabad Locations, Annual Averages*

| Location | Parameters | 2006 | 2007 | 2008 | 2009 | 2010 |
|---|---|---|---|---|---|---|
| Naroda GIDC | $SO_2$ | 13.17 | 16.75 | 12.83 | 17.42 | 19.50 |
| | $NO_2$ | 26.83 | 30.50 | 21.17 | 21.92 | 26.00 |
| | SPM | 331.08 | 351.50 | 331.58 | 297.42 | 381.92 |
| | RSPM | 143.92 | 150.42 | 133.67 | 128.92 | 160.42 |
| Cadila Laboratories | $SO_2$ | 12.00 | 14.58 | 12.42 | 18.75 | 15.58 |
| | $NO_2$ | 24.75 | 25.92 | 20.42 | 23.33 | 20.83 |
| | SPM | 269.92 | 235.67 | 203.58 | 200.42 | 190.50 |
| | RSPM | 83.83 | 101.17 | 81.83 | 90.58 | 86.25 |
| L.D. Engineering College | $SO_2$ | 9.17 | 8.83 | 12.17 | 13.33 | 11.92 |
| | $NO_2$ | 18.67 | 14.42 | 18.17 | 18.25 | 17.00 |
| | SPM | 205.08 | 136.67 | 175.25 | 182.50 | 149.83 |
| | RSPM | 91.83 | 60.33 | 70.00 | 81.42 | 70.00 |
| Shardaben Hospital | $SO_2$ | 10.50 | 12.33 | 12.42 | 14.33 | 13.92 |
| | $NO_2$ | 21.42 | 19.50 | 19.00 | 19.67 | 18.83 |
| | SPM | 205.08 | 195.50 | 204.25 | 194.92 | 183.58 |
| | RSPM | 91.83 | 84.17 | 79.42 | 88.08 | 82.17 |
| R.C. Tech High School | $SO_2$ | 11.33 | 11.50 | 11.75 | 14.83 | 15.25 |
| | $NO_2$ | 22.08 | 19.17 | 19.75 | 19.58 | 20.00 |
| | SPM | 224.00 | 195.33 | 196.50 | 193.58 | 184.33 |
| | RSPM | 102.08 | 83.92 | 80.25 | 88.17 | 92.58 |
| Behrampura Referral Hospital | $SO_2$ | 9.92 | 11.25 | 12.17 | 16.08 | 15.08 |
| | $NO_2$ | 21.33 | 19.25 | 19.25 | 20.67 | 20.00 |
| | SPM | 206.92 | 196.83 | 193.08 | 191.58 | 181.00 |
| | RSPM | 90.92 | 85.25 | 80.33 | 86.00 | 86.33 |
| Mukesh Industries | $SO_2$ | | 19.55 | 14.75 | 18.83 | 20.25 |
| | $NO_2$ | | 33.91 | 22.50 | 23.50 | 26.75 |
| | SPM | | 537.36 | 492.33 | 407.58 | 459.42 |
| | RSPM | | 214.27 | 170.25 | 174.17 | 189.33 |
| Naroda, S.P. Ring Road | $SO_2$ | | 9.45 | 11.42 | 14.08 | 13.25 |
| | $NO_2$ | | 14.64 | 17.75 | 19.17 | 17.83 |
| | SPM | | 155.73 | 178.17 | 194.75 | 173.42 |
| | RSPM | | 80.09 | 74.08 | 86.25 | 84.67 |
| Nava Vadaj | $SO_2$ | | 9.73 | 11.92 | 14.50 | 14.33 |
| | $NO_2$ | | 15.73 | 18.58 | 19.67 | 18.42 |
| | SPM | | 164.73 | 191.83 | 195.67 | 189.25 |
| | RSPM | | 82.18 | 79.00 | 86.08 | 89.50 |

*contd...*

...contd...

| Location | Parameters | 2006 | 2007 | 2008 | 2009 | 2010 |
|---|---|---|---|---|---|---|
| Satellite | $SO_2$ | | 9.40 | 12.00 | 14.75 | 14.58 |
| | $NO_2$ | | 14.90 | 18.50 | 20.42 | 20.33 |
| | SPM | | 170.70 | 192.25 | 198.08 | 171.50 |
| | RSPM | | 76.00 | 80.67 | 88.50 | 81.42 |
| Vatva-Odhav, S.P. Ring Road | $SO_2$ | | 10.45 | 12.08 | 13.92 | 13.67 |
| | $NO_2$ | | 15.73 | 18.58 | 19.17 | 18.33 |
| | SPM | | 179.82 | 192.42 | 189.00 | 179.17 |
| | RSPM | | 79.18 | 78.83 | 84.17 | 85.00 |

Following the Supreme Court identification, the CPCB (Central Pollution Control Board) monitors air quality in 17 cities and Ahmedabad figures in that list. The data are somewhat dated.[9] This report mentions that 85 per cent of urban CO (carbon monoxide) emissions are due to petrol-driven vehicles, 35-65 per cent of unburnt hydrocarbons are due to 2 and 3-wheelers and 90 per cent of NOx (nitrogen oxide) emissions are because of diesel-driven vehicles. Air pollution results from industrial and vehicular sources and coal-fired hearths in slums, small bakeries, roasting centres and small refineries of precious metals. The report then goes on to highlight action taken against 3-wheelers that mix kerosene with petrol and reduction and relocation of industrial pollution. 3-wheelers have also switched to LPG (liquified petroleum gas)/CNG. In the last seven years, in Ahmedabad, an estimated 3,60,000 3-wheelers have completed this switch. The gas grid has enabled domestic consumers and industrial users to switch to gas. Though dated, the data show a discernible reduction in $SO_2$, $NO_2$, SPM and RSPM levels.[10] While data remains a problem, what is true of Ahmedabad should also be true of other cities in Gujarat, with availability of power and switch away from generating sets and others forms of polluting energy, emphasis on renewable sources of energy, improvements in energy efficiency, public transport and reduction in industrial pollution. For example, bus rapid transit systems are estimated to switch 40 per cent of personal vehicular transport to public transport. The energy efficiency programme in municipal corporations and municipalities is estimated to have led to an energy-saving of 30 per cent. In an earlier chapter, we have talked about the power sector and the emphasis

9. Central Pollution Control Board (2006). *Air Quality Trends and Action Plan for Control of Air Pollution from Seventeen Cities*. September. *http://cpcb.nic.in/upload/NewItems/NewItem_104_airquality17cities-package-.pdf.*

10. The development of the Sabarmati river front is specific to Ahmedabad.

on renewable energy. In 2012-13, 7 per cent of Gujarat's power was through RPOs (renewable purchase obligations), 5.50 per cent wind, 1 per cent solar and 0.50 per cent accounted for by others. [11]

One should mention the Nirmal Gujarat Mission too, launched in 2007, focussing on cleanliness, the environment and public health. This has several different components—managing waste in industries, transportation and hospitals; protecting water bodies, trees, green spaces and heritage buildings; capacity-building; creating public awareness; and bringing about behavioural changes. This is not only about urban Gujarat. For example, there are community-managed DEWATS (Decentralised Wastewater Treatment Systems), which also encourage local people in rural areas to build their own toilets, and there is also a campaign against open defecation. In earlier chapters, we have referred to participatory watershed management and the IWDP (Integrated Watershed Development Programme). For monitoring water quality, GPCB has a GEMS (Global Environment Monitoring System) project for major rivers like Narmada, Tapi, Mahi and Sabarmati and a MINARS (Monitoring of Indian National Aquatic Resources System) project for rivers like Sabarmati, Meshwo, Anas, Mahi, Panam, Narmada, Damanganga, Kolak, Par, Tapi and Ambica, not just for river water quality, but also for groundwater quality and lake water quality. In talking about water quality, it is possible to get bogged down in a maze of detail, not only because there are several different variables and several different geographical locations, but also because there is a difference in water quality across rivers, canals, creeks, lakes, tanks, ponds and groundwater. The CPCB brought out a status report on the quality of water in 2010.[12] Because of the different parameters that can be used, different geographical locations and different types of water bodies, it is difficult to deduce much in the nature of trends. This is equally true of trends over time.[13] While it is obvious that water is more available and groundwater levels have gone up, improvements in the quality of water tend to be much more localised. The Central Ground Water Board shows a rise in groundwater levels in Gujarat, though this is subject to some regional variations within the State.[14]

Given Gujarat's growth, much more remarkable has been the increase in forest cover. Since the National Forest Policy of 1988, forestry management

---

11. *op. cit.* no.5.

12. Central Pollution Control Board (2010). *Status of Water Quality in India, 2010. http://www.indiaenvironmentportal.org.in/files/file/WQSTATUS_REPORT2010.pdf*

13. See, for example, the data in annual reports of GPCB, *http://www.gpcb.gov.in/pdf/AR_2011_12_ENG.PDF*

14. See, for example, Central Ground Water Board (2010). *Groundwater Scenario of India, 2009-10.* June. *http://www.cgwb.gov.in/documents/Ground%20Water%20Year%20Book%202009-10.pdf*

**Table 11.2**

*JFM*

| *District* | *Division* | *No. of JFMCs* | *Forest area under JFM* |
|---|---|---|---|
| Rajpipla (East) | Narmada | 184 | 18848.00 |
| Rajpipla(West) | Surat | 149 | 15296.00 |
| Bharuch | Bharuch | 61 | 5762.00 |
| Vyara | Tapi | 183 | 41160.00 |
| Valsad (N) | Valsad | 94 | 5910.40 |
| | Navsari | 70 | 3457.19 |
| Valsad (S) | Valsad | 130 | 14100.05 |
| Dang (N) | Dang | 128 | 8592.81 |
| Dang (S) | Dang | 117 | 4122.08 |
| Baria | Dohad | 283 | 36751.67 |
| Godhra | Panchmahal | 462 | 59113.98 |
| Chhotaudepur | Vadodara | 324 | 57639.60 |
| Surendranagar | Surendranagar | 65 | 11795.73 |
| Jamnagar | Jamnagar | 55 | 14999.00 |
| Bhavnagar | Bhavnagar | 50 | 8705.00 |
| Rajkot | Rajkot | 57 | 5976.00 |
| Junagadh | Junagadh | 66 | 3750.00 |
| | Porbander | 8 | 1125.00 |
| Sabarkantha | Sabarkantha | 149 | 13280.46 |
| Sabarkantha(S) | Sabarkantha | 291 | 21362.75 |
| Banaskantha | Banaskantha | 108 | 7791.13 |
| Gandhinagar | Gandhinagar | 6 | 254.00 |
| | Mahesana | 12 | 1600.66 |
| | Kheda | 9 | 300.00 |
| Kutch (West) | Kutch | 99 | 31900.00 |
| Kutch (East) | Kutch | 44 | 21500.00 |
| Patan | Patan | 25 | 2200.00 |
| Gir (W) | Junagadh | 12 | 3353.72 |
| Nadiad | Kheda | 22 | 4918.01 |
| Total | | 3262 | 425565.24 |
| Gir (E) | | 12 | 3932.62 |
| Total | | 3274 | 429497.86 |

in Gujarat has gone through different stages and the forests are territorially divided into 20 forest divisions and 2 sub-divisions, with separate working plans for these. JFM (Joint Forest Management) has earlier been mentioned and this was introduced in 1991, made applicable to degraded forest areas.

Table 11.2 shows the status of present JFM committees and some of the Vana Kalyan Samitis have won awards.[15] There are different types of forests—reserved forests, protected forests and unclassed forests. What is interesting about Gujarat is the steady increase in forest cover, shown in Table 11.3.[16] That last figure, of 1,833 thousand hectares, is from the latest forest survey of India and amounts to 9.72 per cent of Gujarat's land area.[17] Despite the extraction of timber, fuel-wood and bamboo, and commercial exploitation of NTFP (non-timber forest products) and pressures of development and urbanisation, this increase in forest cover is not something one would have expected *a priori*. In addition to traditional forests, 25,000 hectares of mangrove forests have been added in coastal areas. These are carbon sinks and absorb an estimated 50 tonnes of carbon per hectare.

Nor is this about forests alone. Van Mahotsavs have been held in different parts of the state. Earlier, in 2003 and 2009, there were surveys in the state to count trees outside forests, but in rural areas. In 2011, such a survey was done for municipal corporations and municipalities. Table 11.4 shows what this survey found.[18] There are similar figures for the municipalities too. There is a target that, for mega-cities with a million plus population, the tree cover should be at least 15 per cent of the geographical area. While this may be difficult, Gujarat has an explicit target of achieving 10 per cent.

**Table 11.3**

*Forest Area*

| | *(thousand hectares)* |
|---|---|
| 1991 | 1,190 |
| 1993 | 1,204 |
| 1995 | 1,232 |
| 1997 | 1,258 |
| 1999 | 1,297 |
| 2001 | 1,291 |
| 2003 | 1,482 |
| 2005 | 1,472 |
| 2011 | 1,833 |

**Table 11.4**

*Tree Population in Municipal Corporation Areas*

| *Area* | *Tree Density Per Hectare* | *Tree Cover as % of Geographical Area* |
|---|---|---|
| Ahmedabad | 13.2 | 4.66 |
| Surat | 8.4 | 3.00 |
| Vadodara | 45.9 | 16.29 |
| Gandhinagar | 152.0 | 53.9 |
| Rajkot | 13.2 | 4.69 |
| Bhavnagar + Victoria Park | 89.46 | 21.35 |
| Junagadh | 13.5 | 4.80 |
| Jamnagar | 13.4 | 4.74 |

15. *http://www.gujaratforest.org/formgm-pres-status.htm*
16. *http://www.gujaratforest.org/forests-for_cover.htm*
17. *http://fsi.org.in/cover_2011/gujrat.pdf*
18. Gujarat Forest Department (2012). *Status of Tree Cover in Urban Areas of Gujarat.*

Gujarat also has several wildlife sanctuaries in Gir, Vansda, Nal Sarovar, Jessore, Barda, Hingolgadh, Narayan Sarovar, Khijadia, Ratanmahal, Kutch, Gaga, Rampara, Thol, Shoolpaneshwar, Porbandar, Pania, Jambughoda, Purna, and so on. This is not the place to discuss these, or to discuss the links these have with tourism. However, it is worth mentioning that conservation efforts have led to an increase in the number of wildlife, despite the trade-offs with development. For example, the last census shows an estimated 411 lions in Gir. But the number has increased and is believed to be higher.

It is easy to get bogged down in detail. However, the big picture is a simple one. With the emphasis on growth and industrialisation, it would have been easy for Gujarat to pay scant attention to the environment. Especially since the Eleventh Five Year Plan (2007-2012), this is not quite what has happened. There is increased attention to protecting the environment and sustainable development. If there is a trade-off between the two objectives, and that proposition can be contested, Gujarat has not accepted the trade-off.

# 12

# Epilogue

Gujarat has a vision of attaining upper middle income status by 2020. At least, that is the implicit message of the BIG report. Without getting into digressions about PPP (purchasing power parity) *versus* official exchange rates, upper middle income status is defined by the World Bank today, as a per capita income of more than $4,036, in today's dollars and using official exchange rates.[1] While per capita GSDP is not the same as per capita income, and conversions are subject to exchange rates used, Gujarat's per capita GSDP in 2010-11 is roughly around 876 US dollars.[2] Future projections are dependent on assumptions about inflation rates and exchange rates. As India grows, PPP considerations imply that the rupee should appreciate against the US dollar. If both inflation and exchange rate appreciation are ignored, in today's dollars, even a 10 per cent growth over the next decade does not get Gujarat to a per capita income of over 4,000 US dollars. The figure is likely to be more like 2,300 US dollars. But that is in today's dollars. An inflation of the order of 5 per cent and an exchange rate appreciation of the order of 1.5 per cent of course takes Gujarat to the threshold of a per capita income of $ 4,000, even with a slightly lower rate of growth of around 8 per cent.

Can the present rate of growth of 10 per cent be sustained? Several people have done forecasts for the Indian economy. In rare cases, like the first Goldman-Sachs report,[3] these involve an estimation of Cobb-Douglas production functions. Stated simply, this involves a decomposition of output growth into a labour component, a capital component and a residual that can be interpreted as TFP (total factor productivity) growth. At low levels of economic development, growth is often extensive, with output increases resulting from increases in capital and labour. At higher levels of economic development, the focus needs to shift to intensive growth, with output increases resulting from greater efficiencies with which inputs (including natural resources) are used. This shows up as productivity increases. Cobb-Douglas production functions have not been estimated for Indian states. Data limitations stand in the way. However, the principle is easily understood. While productivity increases resulting from better physical and social infrastructure have also been important for Gujarat, much of that 10 per cent growth has come from increases in capital and labour, although decomposition is difficult. Gujarat's decadal rate of population growth from 2001 to 2011 is slightly misleading, since it masks a slowing down of population growth. While one should not push the point too hard, Gujarat already faces a labour shortage in some

1. *http://data.worldbank.org/about/country-classifications*

2. CSO's 2010-11 per capita GSDP numbers converted, using an exchange rate of 54 rupees to 1 US dollar.

3. Wilson, Dominic and Roopa Purushothaman (2003). "Dreaming with BRICs: The Path to 2050", *Global Economics Paper* No.99. Goldman Sachs. October 1.

segments and in-migration has declined,[4] a reflection of better economic opportunities in other states. As Table 12.1 shows, in the 25-54 age-group, work-force participation rates in Gujarat are already quite high, especially among males.[5] Economic development generally leads to an increase in female work-force participation rates. There are several interventions that are directed specifically at women. For example, in 2006, a Nari Gaurav Niti, a State policy for gender equity, was announced. The specific targets on social sectors (education, health), housing and governance or the agenda on gender empowerment and gender neutrality can be glossed over, the simple point being that increased participation of women in economic activities can neutralise labour shortage disadvantages, as can increases in life expectancy and improvements in the quality of labour inputs.

**Table 12.1**

*Work Force Participation Rate, 25-54 Years*

| *District* | *Male* | *Female* | *Total* |
|---|---|---|---|
| Jamnagar | 92.78 | 21.33 | 58.15 |
| Rajkot | 91.91 | 22.79 | 58.11 |
| Surendranagar | 93.92 | 28.44 | 62.68 |
| Bhavnagar | 98.35 | 29.81 | 65.07 |
| Amreli | 97.75 | 24.57 | 61.51 |
| Junagadh | 90.92 | 20.96 | 56.78 |
| Kachch | 94.01 | 24.33 | 59.74 |
| Banaskantha | 97.72 | 20.15 | 60.30 |
| Sabarkantha | 92.24 | 28.74 | 60.60 |
| Mahesana | 91.51 | 23.93 | 58.26 |
| Gandhinagar | 82.21 | 14.25 | 49.70 |
| Ahmedabad | 84.49 | 15.15 | 51.84 |
| Kheda | 91.16 | 19.90 | 57.01 |
| Panchmahal | 94.91 | 27.11 | 62.10 |
| Vadodara | 90.34 | 20.58 | 57.33 |
| Bharuch | 93.29 | 29.62 | 63.04 |
| Surat | 95.09 | 30.20 | 65.04 |
| Valsad | 92.13 | 32.89 | 63.16 |
| Dangs | 82.14 | 62.73 | 72.56 |
| **Gujarat** | **92.06** | **23.95** | **59.27** |

4. In the 2001 Census, 5.1 per cent of Gujarat's population consisted of in-migrants. *http://censusindia.gov.in/Data_Products/Data_Highlights/Data_Highlights_link/data_highlights_D1D2D3.pdf*

5. *Gujarat Social Infrastructure Vision 2010. http://www.talimrojgar.org/pages/statistics.pdf*

Having said this, the point about growth impulses resulting from greater productivity and improved efficiencies in input usage (labour, capital and natural resources) remains. This is one reason why growth is easier at lower levels of economic development and peters out as one moves up the development ladder. Cross-country experience is replete with examples of countries that fail to cross the so-called middle income trap. This does not contradict the slack that remains in the present system. A few back-of-the-envelope figures will illustrate what one means. Agricultural transformation throughout the state can add an incremental 1 per cent to GDP growth. Physical infrastructure throughout the state can add an increment of another 1 per cent and the increment from satisfactory delivery of public services is also of the same order. Therefore, for the next decade, 10 per cent GSDP growth is doable, but it increasingly becomes difficult. This is all the more because at higher levels of economic development, the protection of the environment attains a higher priority. The state government has initiatives for protecting the environment, such as farm forestry, industrial afforestation, energy conservation, bio-fertiliser and bio-pesticide use, green buildings, solar piping and lighting, eco-industrial estates and implementation of the polluter paying principle.[6] These initiatives have been documented in detail in Chapter 11. While the agenda is unassailable and is part of a sustainable development plan, protecting the environment is partly a function of decentralisation of property rights and partly a function of appropriate prices that internalise costs of negative externalities associated with environmental degradation. *Ipso facto*, there are trade-offs, even if these are conscious ones. Therefore, even if the target for the next decade is real GSDP growth of 10 per cent, even 8 per cent and more would be a remarkable accomplishment.

To return to the Gujarat story or Gujarat model mentioned in the Prologue, is there a Gujarat story? Clearly, there is. That is reflected in high GSDP growth since 2002 and is also reflected in poverty declines, with no significant increase in inequality, data constraints notwithstanding. Is this reflected in human development outcomes improving, especially in backward geographical regions and backward segments of the population? The evidence suggests that there have been improvements, especially after the conscious focus on such regions and segments since the Eleventh Plan (2007-2012). Therefore, if Gujarat is being criticised on inequitable development, the time-line of data points is important. Pre-2007 data are not pertinent and one must also remember that social sector outcomes often improve with a time-lag. At best, one can complain that these improvements are not yet reflected in northern and central Gujarat.

---

6. Also see Modi, Narendra (2011). *Convenient Action: Gujarat's Response to Challenges of Climate Change*. Macmillan Publishers.

If one accepts this Gujarat story, one can move on to the next question. What is the Gujarat model and what has happened? Before answering that, a few more quotes from Swami Vivekananda are relevant. "The grace of both Lakshmi (goddess of fortune) and Sarasvati (goddess of learning) now shines on the peoples of the Western countries. ...We also had that trait once—when there was wealth and prosperity in the land. We have now too much poverty, but, to make matters worse, we are courting our ruin in two ways—namely, we are throwing away what we have as our own, and labouring in vain to make others' ideals and habits ours. ...The Bengal that is to be has not as yet got a stable footing. It is our arts that have fared the worst of all. In the days gone by, our old women used to paint the floors, doors, and walls of their houses with a paste of rice-powder, drawing various beautiful figures; they used to cut plantain leaves in an artistic manner, to serve the food on; they used to lavish their art in nicely arranging the different comestibles on the plates. Those arts, in these days, have gradually disappeared or are doing so."[7] For empowering both Lakshmi and Sarasvati, we have the following. The emphasis was on individual enterprise and initiative. "In these days of dire famine, flood, disease, and pestilence, tell me where your Congressmen are. Will it do merely to say, "Hand the government of the country over to us"? And who is there to listen to them? If a man does work, has he to open his mouth to ask for anything? ...When a great work is being done, when the foundations are laid or a road constructed, when superhuman energy is needed—it is one or two extraordinary men who silently and noiselessly work through a world of obstacles and difficulties."[8] Though not stated that explicitly, there is skepticism in this quote about the role of the state or the government. One also detects that refrain in the following. "The wealth and power of a country are in the hands of a few men who do not work but manipulate the work of millions of human beings. By this power they can deluge the whole earth with blood. Religion and all things are under their feet; they rule and stand supreme. The Western world is governed by a handful of Shylocks. All those things that you hear about—constitutional government, freedom, liberty, and parliaments—are but jokes."[9] Indeed, there are sections on what we would today call, public revenue and public expenditure, not to speak of devolution and decentralisation of decision-making. "To protect the State, to meet the expenses of the personal comforts and luxuries of himself and his long retinue, and, above all, to fill to overflowing the coffers of the all-powerful priesthood for its propitiation, the king is continually draining the resources of his subjects, even as the sun sucks up moisture from the earth. His especial prey—his milch cows—are the Vaishyas. Neither

7. *http://www.ramakrishnavivekananda.info/vivekananda/volume_5/vol_5_frame.htm*

8. *http://www.ramakrishnavivekananda.info/vivekananda/volume_6/vol_6_frame.htm*

9. *http://www.ramakrishnavivekananda.info/vivekananda/volume_3/vol_3_frame.htm*

under the Hindu kings, nor under the Buddhist rule, do we find the common subject-people taking any part in expressing their voice in the affairs of the State. True, Yudhishthira visits the houses of Vaishyas and even Shudras when he is in Vâranâvata; true, the subjects are praying for the installation of Râmachandra to the regency of Ayodhyâ; nay, they are even criticising the conduct of Sitâ and secretly making plans for the bringing about of her exile: but as a recognised rule of the State they have no direct voice in the supreme government. The power of the populace is struggling to express itself in indirect and disorderly ways without any method. The people have not as yet the conscious knowledge of the existence of this power. There is neither the attempt on their part to organise it into a united action, nor have they got the will to do so; there is also a complete absence of that capacity, that skill, by means of which small and incoherent centres of force are united together, creating insuperable strength as their resultant. Is this due to want of proper laws?—no, that is not it. There are laws, there are methods, separately and distinctly assigned for the guidance of different departments of government, there are laws laid down in the minutest detail for everything, such as the collection of revenue, the management of the army, the administration of justice, punishments and rewards. But at the root of all, is the injunction of the Rishi—the word of divine authority, the revelation of God coming through the inspired Rishi. The laws have, it can almost be said, no elasticity in them. Under the circumstances, it is never possible for the people to acquire any sort of education by which they can learn to combine among themselves and be united for the accomplishment of any object for the common good of the people, or by which they can have the concerted intellect to conceive the idea of popular right in the treasures collected by the king from his subjects, or even such education by which they can be fired with the aspiration to gain the right of representation in the control of State revenues and expenditure."[10]

And finally, in a longish quote, there is recognition of what we would today call network effects. "As during the supremacy of the Brahmin and the Kshatriya, there is a centralization of learning and advancement of civilization, so the result of the supremacy of the Vaishya is accumulation of wealth. The power of the Vaishya lies in the possession of that coin, the charm of whose clinking sound works with an irresistible fascination on the minds of the four castes. The Vaishya is always in fear lest the Brahmin swindles him out of this, his only possession, and lest the Kshatriya usurps it by virtue of his superior strength of arms. For self-preservation, the Vaishyas as a body are, therefore, of one mind. The Vaishya commands the money; the exorbitant interest that he can exact for its use by others, as with a lash in his hand, is his powerful weapon which strikes terror in the heart

10. *http://www.ramakrishnavivekananda.info/vivekananda/volume_4/vol_4_frame.htm*

of all. By the power of his money, he is always busy curbing the royal power. That the royal power may not anyhow stand in the way of the inflow of his riches, the merchant is ever watchful. But, for all that, he has never the least wish that the power should pass on from the kingly to the Shudra class. ...And where are they through whose physical labour only are possible the influence of the Brahmin, the prowess of the Kshatriya, and the fortune of the Vaishya? What is their history, who, being the real body of society, are designated at all times in all countries as 'baseborn'?—for whom kind India prescribed the mild punishments, 'Cut out his tongue, chop off his flesh', and others of like nature, for such a grave offence as any attempt on their part to gain a share of the knowledge and wisdom monopolised by her higher classes—those 'moving corpses' of India and the 'beasts of burden' of other countries—the Shudras, what is their lot in life? What shall I say of India? Let alone her Shudra class, her Brahmins to whom belonged the acquisition of scriptural knowledge are now the foreign professors, her Kshatriyas the ruling Englishmen, and Vaishyas, too, the English in whose bone and marrow is the instinct of trade, so that, only the Shudra-ness—the-beast-of-burdenness—is now left with the Indians themselves...In spite of the spread of education in the West, there is a great hindrance in the way of the rising of the Shudra class, and that is the recognition of caste as determined by the inherence of more or less good or bad qualities. By this very qualitative caste system which obtained in India in ancient days, the Shudra class was kept down, bound hand and foot. In the first place, scarcely any opportunity was given to the Shudra for the accumulation of wealth or the earning of proper knowledge and education; to add to this disadvantage, if ever a man of extraordinary parts and genius were born of the Shudra class, the influential higher sections of the society forthwith showered titular honours on him and lifted him up to their own circle. His wealth and the power of his wisdom were employed for the benefit of an alien caste—and his own caste-people reaped no benefits of his attainments; and not only so, the good-for-nothing people, the scum and refuse of the higher castes, were cast off and thrown into the Shudra class to swell their number. ..In modern India, no one born of Shudra parents, be he a millionaire or a great Pandit, has ever the right to leave his own society, with the result that the power of his wealth, intellect, or wisdom, remaining confined within his own caste limits, is being employed for the betterment of his own community. This hereditary caste system of India, being thus unable to overstep its own bounds, is slowly but surely conducing to the advancement of the people moving within the same circle. The improvement of the lower classes of India will go on, in this way, so long as India will be under a government dealing with its subjects irrespective of their caste and position."[11]

11. *http://www.ramakrishnavivekananda.info/vivekananda/volume_4/vol_4_frame.htm*

What is the Gujarat model then? It is one of freeing up space for private initiative and enterprise and the creation of an enabling environment by the state. It is one of decentralisation of planning and empowering people. It is about targeted public expenditure through specific schemes, supplementing CSSs with state-specific schemes. It is one of bureaucratic empowerment and improving the efficiency of public expenditure. It is one of feedback loops from the government machinery to people and from people to the government machinery. It is one of delivering public goods (water, roads, electricity, schools, education). Stated thus, this is a standard development template that any state ought to adopt and implement. The difference is that not too many states have implemented the template. It is always difficult to disentangle the various factors that go into ensuring the successful implementation of the Gujarat model. First, there is a legacy factor and earlier Gujarat governments, prior to 2002, have left positive impact. Second, Gujarat has had a healthy tradition of private entrepreneurship and an equally healthy skepticism of government. Third, in sectors like water and roads, Gujarat has also benefitted from favourable exogenous circumstances, as it has from negative push factors in other states, automobiles and auto ancillaries being an obvious instance. Fourth, the present political leadership has also had a role in empowering the bureaucracy, clamping down on corruption, decentralising planning and delivery and focussed intervention for backward regions and segments. While disentangling is difficult, it would be uncharitable and unfair to deny this fourth element. To put it even more strongly, this would violate the facts and be dishonest. The pride in 'asmita' begins from the top. And if that is disseminated and successfully trickles down, quite a bit has been achieved.

*About the Author:*

**Bibek Debroy** is Professor at the Centre for Policy Research (Delhi), Contributing Editor with The Economic Times and Visiting Honorary Senior Research Fellow, Institute for South Asian Studies (ISAS), National University of Singapore. In the past, he has worked in universities, research institutes and management schools, and for an industry chamber and for the government. He is the author of several popular articles, academic papers and books.